Cram101 Textbook Outlines to accompany:

Understanding Motor Development

Gallahue and Ozmun, 5th Edition

An Academic Internet Publishers (AIPI) publication (c) 2007.

You have a discounted membership at www.Cram101.com with this book.

Get all of the practice tests for the chapters of this textbook, and access in-depth reference material for writing essays and papers. Here is an example from a Cram101 Biology text:

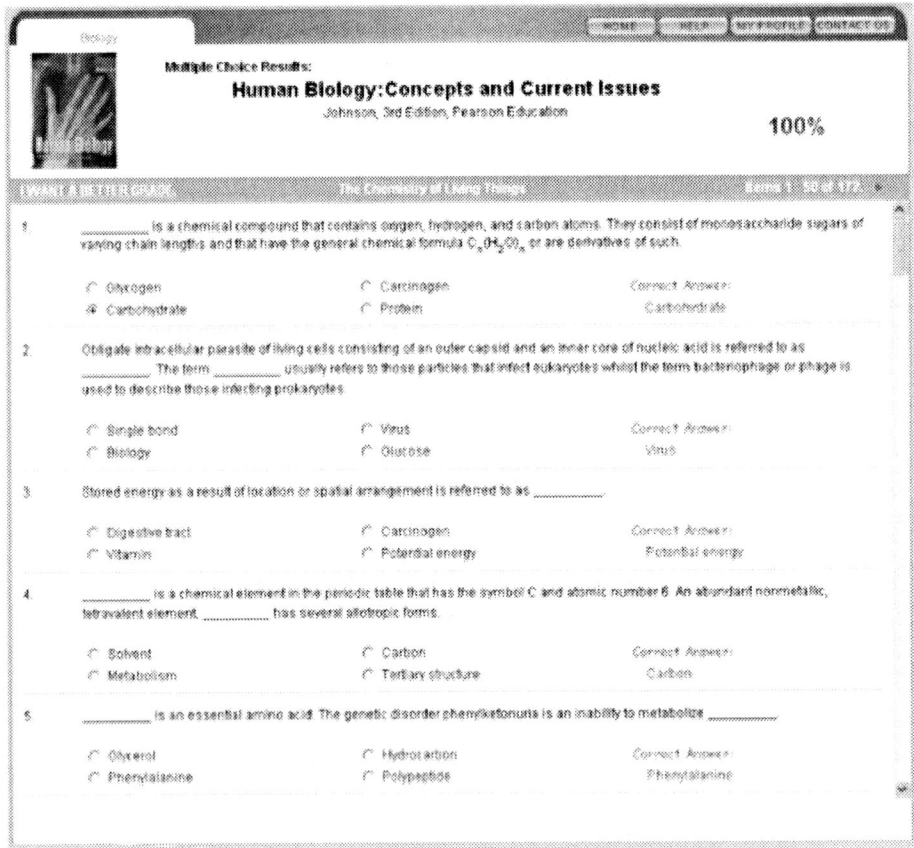

When you need problem solving help with math, stats, and other disciplines, www.Cram101.com will walk through the formulas and solutions step by step.

With Cram101.com online, you also have access to extensive reference material.

You will nail those essays and papers. Here is an example from a Cram101 Biology text:

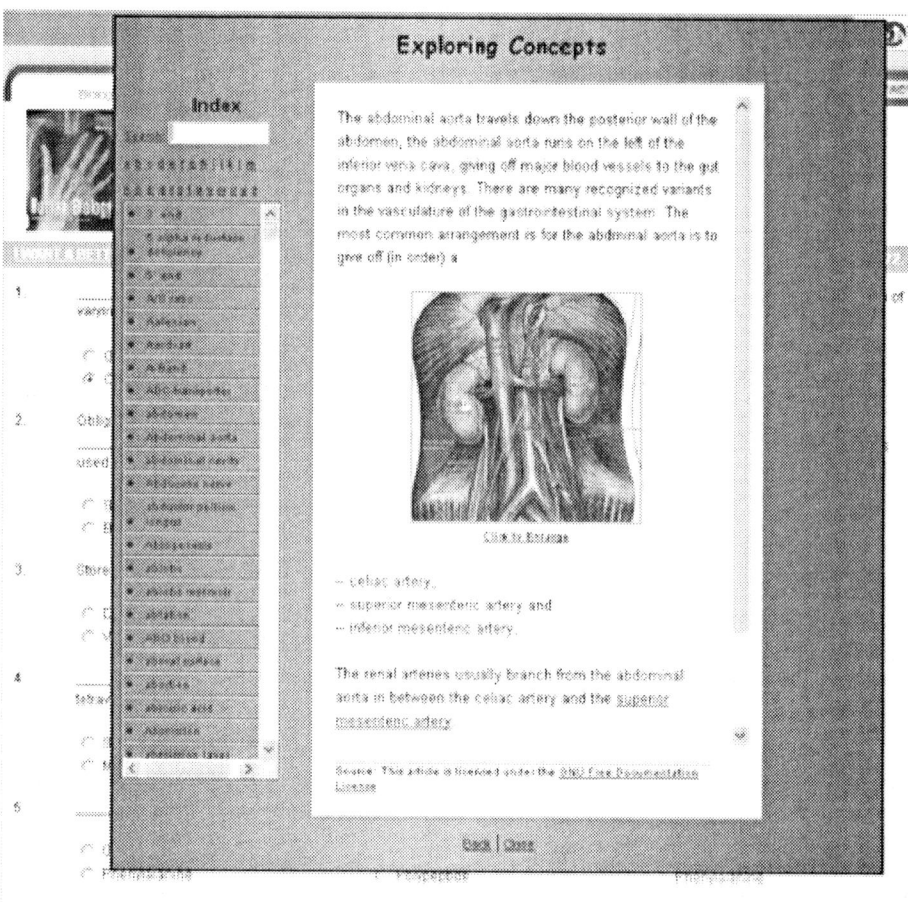

Visit **www.Cram101.com**, click Sign Up at the top of the screen, and enter DK73DW in the promo code box on the registration screen. Access to www.Cram101.com is normally $9.95, but because you have purchased this book, your access fee is only $4.95. Sign up and stop highlighting textbooks forever.

Learning System

Cram101 Textbook Outlines is a learning system. The notes in this book are the highlights of your textbook, you will never have to highlight a book again.

How to use this book. Take this book to class, it is your notebook for the lecture. The notes and highlights on the left hand side of the pages follow the outline and order of the textbook. All you have to do is follow along while your intructor presents the lecture. Circle the items emphasized in class and add other important information on the right side. With Cram101 Textbook Outlines you'll spend less time writing and more time listening. Learning becomes more efficient.

Cram101.com Online

Increase your studying efficiency by using Cram101.com's practice tests and online reference material. It is the perfect complement to Cram101 Textbook Outlines. Use self-teaching matching tests or simulate in-class testing with comprehensive multiple choice tests, or simply use Cram's true and false tests for quick review. Cram101.com even allows you to enter your in-class notes for an integrated studying format combining the textbook notes with your class notes.

Understanding Motor Development
Gallahue and Ozmun, 5th

CONTENTS

Chronological age	Chronological age refers to the number of years that have elapsed since a person's birth.
Learning	Learning is a relatively permanent change in behavior that results from experience. Thus, to attribute a behavioral change to learning, the change must be relatively permanent and must result from experience.
Affective	Affective is the way people react emotionally, their ability to feel another living thing's pain or
Developmental psychologist	A psychologist interested in human growth and development from conception until death is referred to as a developmental psychologist.
Developmental psychology	The branch of psychology that studies the patterns of growth and change occurring throughout life is referred to as developmental psychology.
Social psychology	Social psychology is the study of the nature and causes of human social behavior, with an emphasis on how people think towards each other and how they relate to each other.
Physiology	The study of the functions and activities of living cells, tissues, and organs and of the physical and chemical phenomena involved is referred to as physiology.
Causation	Causation concerns the time order relationship between two or more objects such that if a specific antecendent condition occurs the same consequent must always follow.
Heredity	Heredity is the transfer of characteristics from parent to offspring through their genes.
Transactional model	Transactional model refers to a framework that views development as the continuous and bidirectional interchange between an active organism with a unique biological constitution, and a changing environment.
Life span	Life span refers to the upper boundary of life, the maximum number of years an individual can live. The maximum life span of human beings is about 120 years of age. Females live an average of 6 years longer than males.
Stages	Stages represent relatively discrete periods of time in which functioning is qualitatively different from functioning at other periods.
Adolescence	The period of life bounded by puberty and the assumption of adult responsibilities is adolescence.
Infancy	The developmental period that extends from birth to 18 or 24 months is called infancy.
Individuality	According to Cooper, individuality consists of two dimensions: self-assertion and separateness.
Acquisition	Acquisition is the process of adapting to the environment, learning or becoming conditioned. In classical conditoning terms, it is the initial learning of the stimulus response link, which involves a neutral stimulus being associated with a unconditioned stimulus and becoming a conditioned stimulus.
Arnold Gesell	Arnold Gesell was a pioneer in the field of child development and developmental measurement. He constructed the Gesell dome, a one-way mirror shaped as a dome, under which children could be observed without being disturbed.
Cognitive development	The process by which a child's understanding of the world changes as a function of age and experience is called cognitive development.
Maturation	The orderly unfolding of traits, as regulated by the genetic code is called maturation.
Knowledge base	The general background information a person possesses, which influences most cognitive task performance is called the knowledge base.
Dynamic Systems Theory	Dynamic Systems Theory believes that in order to develop motor skills, infants must perceive something in the environment that motivates them to act, and they must use their perceptions to fine-tune their movements. Motor skills represent solutions to the infant's goals. The behavior is the result of many converging factors.

Normative	The term normative is used to describe the effects of those structures of culture which regulate the function of social activity.
Longitudinal approach	The Longitudinal approach is a research strategy in which the same individuals are studied over a period of time, usually several years or more.
Variable	A variable refers to a measurable factor, characteristic, or attribute of an individual or a system.
Longitudinal study	Longitudinal study refers to a type of developmental study in which the same group of participants is followed and measured at different ages on some set of behaviors.
Longitudinal studies	Investigation that collects information on the same individuals repeatedly over time, perhaps over many years, in an effort to determine how phenomena change is referred to as longitudinal studies. These studies to to be time consuming and expensive.
Down syndrome	Down syndrome encompasses a number of genetic disorders, of which trisomy 21 (a nondisjunction, the so-called extrachromosone) is the most representative, causing highly variable degrees of learning difficulties as well as physical disabilities. Incidence of Down syndrome is estimated at 1 per 660 births, making it the most common chromosomal abnormality.
Reliability	Reliability means the extent to which a test produces a consistent , reproducible score .
Cross-sectional study	A type of developmental study in which researchers compare groups of participants of different ages on certain characteristics to determine age related differences is called a cross-sectional study.
Representative sample	Representative sample refers to a sample of participants selected from the larger population in such a way that important subgroups within the population are included in the sample in the same proportions as they are found in the larger population.
Random selection	Choosing a sample so that each member of the population has an equal chance of being included in the sample is called random selection.
Population	Population refers to all members of a well-defined group of organisms, events, or things.
Cross-sectional approach	A research strategy in which individuals of different ages are compared at one time is a cross-sectional approach.
Longitudinal research	Research that studies the same subjects over an extended period of time, usually several years or more, is called longitudinal research.
Naturalistic observation	Naturalistic observation is a method of observation that involves observing subjects in their natural habitats. Researchers take great care in avoiding making interferences with the behavior they are observing by using unobtrusive methods.
Interrater reliability	Interrater reliability is the correlation between ratings of two or more raters in a given research study.
Validity	The extent to which a test measures what it is intended to measure is called validity.
Research design	A research design tests a hypothesis. The basic typess are: descriptive, correlational, and experimental.
Developmental level	An individual's current state of physical, emotional, and intellectual development is called the developmental level.
Biological age	A person's age based on the relative age of their organs is called their biological age. The younger the person's biological age, the longer the life expectancy, regardless of chronological age.
Socialization	Social rules and social relations are created, communicated, and changed in verbal and nonverbal ways creating social complexity useful in identifying outsiders and intelligent breeding partners. The process of learning these skills is called socialization.
Mental age	The mental age refers to the accumulated months of credit that a person earns on the Stanford-Binet

	Intelligence Scale.
Self-concept	Self-concept refers to domain-specific evaluations of the self where a domain may be academics, athletics, etc.
Qualitative change	A qualitative change refers to a change in kind, structure, or organization, such as the change from nonverbal to verbal communication.
Innate	Innate behavior is not learned or influenced by the environment, rather, it is present or predisposed at birth.
Affect	A subjective feeling or emotional tone often accompanied by bodily expressions noticeable to others is called affect.
Regression	Return to a form of behavior characteristic of an earlier stage of development is called regression.
Central nervous system	The vertebrate central nervous system consists of the brain and spinal cord.
Motor cortex	Motor cortex refers to the section of cortex that lies in the frontal lobe, just across the central fissure from the sensory cortex. Neural impulses in the motor cortex are linked to muscular responses throughout the body.
Brain	The brain controls and coordinates most movement, behavior and homeostatic body functions such as heartbeat, blood pressure, fluid balance and body temperature. Functions of the brain are responsible for cognition, emotion, memory, motor learning and other sorts of learning. The brain is primarily made up of two types of cells: glia and neurons.
Plato	According to Plato, people must come equipped with most of their knowledge and need only hints and contemplation to complete it. Plato suggested that the brain is the mechanism of mental processes and that one gained knowledge by reflecting on the contents of one's mind.
Piaget	Piaget argued that young children's answers were qualitatively different than older children rather than quantitative. There are two major aspects to his theory: the process of coming to know and the stages we move through as we gradually acquire this ability.
Skeletal muscle	Skeletal muscle is a type of striated muscle, attached to the skeleton. They are used to facilitate movement, by applying force to bones and joints; via contraction. They generally contract voluntarily (via nerve stimulation), although they can contract involuntarily.
Perception	Perception is the process of acquiring, interpreting, selecting, and organizing sensory information.
Emotion	An emotion is a mental states that arise spontaneously, rather than through conscious effort. They are often accompanied by physiological changes.
Self-worth	In psychology, self-esteem or self-worth refers to a person's subjective appraisal of himself or herself as intrinsically positive or negative to some degree.
Sensorimotor	The first of Piaget's stages is the Sensorimotor stage. This stage typically ranges from birth to 2 years. In this stage, children experience the world through their senses. During this stage, object permanence and stranger anxiety develop.
Cognition	The intellectual processes through which information is obtained, transformed, stored, retrieved, and otherwise used is cognition.
Reinforcement	In operant conditioning, reinforcement is any change in an environment that (a) occurs after the behavior, (b) seems to make that behavior re-occur more often in the future and (c) that reoccurence of behavior must be the result of the change.
Motivation	In psychology, motivation is the driving force (desire) behind all actions of an organism.
Scheme	According to Piaget, a hypothetical mental structure that permits the classification and organization

Go to **Cram101.com** for the Practice Tests for this Chapter.

of new information is called a scheme.

Occupational therapists	Occupational therapists work with the disabled, the elderly, newborns, school-aged children, and with anyone who has a permanent or temporary impairment in their physical or mental functioning.
Gross motor skills	Gross motor skills refer to motor skills that involve large muscle activities, such as walking.
Plasticity	The capacity for modification and change is referred to as plasticity.
Feedback	Feedback refers to information returned to a person about the effects a response has had.
Attention	Attention is the cognitive process of selectively concentrating on one thing while ignoring other things. Psychologists have labeled three types of attention: sustained attention, selective attention, and divided attention.
Variability	Statistically, variability refers to how much the scores in a distribution spread out, away from the mean.
Physical therapy	Physical therapy is a health profession concerned with the assessment, diagnosis, and treatment of disease and disability through physical means. It is based upon principles of medical science, and is generally held to be within the sphere of conventional medicine.

Arnold Gesell	Arnold Gesell was a pioneer in the field of child development and developmental measurement. He constructed the Gesell dome, a one-way mirror shaped as a dome, under which children could be observed without being disturbed.
Sigmund Freud	Sigmund Freud was the founder of the psychoanalytic school, based on his theory that unconscious motives control much behavior, that particular kinds of unconscious thoughts and memories are the source of neurosis, and that neurosis could be treated through bringing these unconscious thoughts and memories to consciousness in psychoanalytic treatment.
Erik Erikson	Erik Erikson conceived eight stages of development, each confronting the individual with its own psychosocial demands, that continued into old age. Personality development, according to Erikson, takes place through a series of crises that must be overcome and internalized by the individual in preparation for the next developmental stage. Such crisis are not catastrophes but vulnerabilities.
Piaget	Piaget argued that young children's answers were qualitatively different than older children rather than quantitative. There are two major aspects to his theory: the process of coming to know and the stages we move through as we gradually acquire this ability.
Attention	Attention is the cognitive process of selectively concentrating on one thing while ignoring other things. Psychologists have labeled three types of attention: sustained attention, selective attention, and divided attention.
Theories	Theories are logically self-consistent models or frameworks describing the behavior of a certain natural or social phenomenon. They are broad explanations and predictions concerning phenomena of interest.
Psychoanalytic	Freud's theory that unconscious forces act as determinants of personality is called psychoanalytic theory. The theory is a developmental theory characterized by critical stages of development.
Psychiatrist	A psychiatrist is a physician who specializes in the diagnosis and treatment of psychological disorders.
Personality	Personality refers to the pattern of enduring characteristics that differentiates a person, the patterns of behaviors that make each individual unique.
Psychosexual stages	In Freudian theory each child passes through five psychosexual stages. During each stage, the id focuses on a distinct erogenous zone on the body. Suffering from trauma during any of the first three stages may result in fixation in that stage. Freud related the resolutions of the stages with adult personalities and personality disorders.
Motives	Needs or desires that energize and direct behavior toward a goal are motives.
Genital stage	The genital stage in psychology is the term used by Sigmund Freud to describe the final stage of human psychosexual development. It is characterized by the expression of libido through intercourse with an adult of the other gender.
Superego	Frued's third psychic structure, which functions as a moral guardian and sets forth high standards for behavior is the superego.
Latency	In child development, latency refers to a phase of psychosexual development characterized by repression of sexual impulses. In learning theory, latency is the delay between stimulus (S) and response (R), which according to Hull depends on the strength of the association.
Ego	In Freud's view the Ego serves to balance our primitive needs and our moral beliefs and taboos. Relying on experience, a healthy Ego provides the ability to adapt to reality and interact with the outside world.
Sensation	Sensation is the first stage in the chain of biochemical and neurologic events that begins

Go to **Cram101.com** for the Practice Tests for this Chapter.

with the impinging of a stimulus upon the receptor cells of a sensory organ, which then leads to perception, the mental state that is reflected in statements like "I see a uniformly blue wall."

Society	The social sciences use the term society to mean a group of people that form a semi-closed (or semi-open) social system, in which most interactions are with other individuals belonging to the group.
Heredity	Heredity is the transfer of characteristics from parent to offspring through their genes.
Stages	Stages represent relatively discrete periods of time in which functioning is qualitatively different from functioning at other periods.
Maturational theory	Gesell's view that development is self-regulated by the unfolding of natural plans and processes is referred to as the maturational theory.
Nervous system	The body's electrochemical communication circuitry, made up of billions of neurons is a nervous system.
Maturation	The orderly unfolding of traits, as regulated by the genetic code is called maturation.
Acquisition	Acquisition is the process of adapting to the environment, learning or becoming conditioned. In classical conditoning terms, it is the initial learning of the stimulus response link, which involves a neutral stimulus being associated with a unconditioned stimulus and becoming a conditioned stimulus.
Infancy	The developmental period that extends from birth to 18 or 24 months is called infancy.
Child development	Scientific study of the processes of change from conception through adolescence is called child development.
Evolution	Commonly used to refer to gradual change, evolution is the change in the frequency of alleles within a population from one generation to the next. This change may be caused by different mechanisms, including natural selection, genetic drift, or changes in population (gene flow).
Cognitive development	The process by which a child's understanding of the world changes as a function of age and experience is called cognitive development.
Cognitive structure	According to Piaget, the number of schemata available to an organism at any given time constitutes that organism's cognitive structure. How the organism interacts with its environment depends on the current cognitive structure available. As the cognitive structure develops, new assimilations can occur.
Chronological age	Chronological age refers to the number of years that have elapsed since a person's birth.
Concrete operations	In Piaget's theory, the third major stage of cognitive development, in which children can decenter their perception, are less egocentric, and can think logically about concrete objects is called concrete operations.
Formal operations	Formal operations in Piaget's theory is the final stage of cognitive development, in which children are able to apply abstract logical rules. Not everyone reaches the formal operations stage of development.
Sensorimotor	The first of Piaget's stages is the Sensorimotor stage. This stage typically ranges from birth to 2 years. In this stage, children experience the world through their senses. During this stage, object permanence and stranger anxiety develop.
Psychosocial development	Erikson's psychosocial development describe eight developmental stages through which a healthily developing human should pass from infancy to late adulthood. In each stage the person confronts, and hopefully masters, new challenges.

Go to **Cram101.com** for the Practice Tests for this Chapter.

Psychosexual development	In psychodynamic theory, the process by which libidinal energy is expressed through different erogenous zones during different stages of development is called psychosexual development.
Life span	Life span refers to the upper boundary of life, the maximum number of years an individual can live. The maximum life span of human beings is about 120 years of age. Females live an average of 6 years longer than males.
Scheme	According to Piaget, a hypothetical mental structure that permits the classification and organization of new information is called a scheme.
Stage theory	Stage theory characterizes development by hypothesizing the existence of distinct, and often critical, periods of life. Each period follows one another in an orderly sequence.
Normative	The term normative is used to describe the effects of those structures of culture which regulate the function of social activity.
Learning disorder	A disorder characterized by a discrepancy between one's academic achievement and one's intellectual ability is referred to as a learning disorder.
Adolescence	The period of life bounded by puberty and the assumption of adult responsibilities is adolescence.
Early childhood	Early childhood refers to the developmental period extending from the end of infancy to about 5 or 6 years of age; sometimes called the preschool years.
Learning	Learning is a relatively permanent change in behavior that results from experience. Thus, to attribute a behavioral change to learning, the change must be relatively permanent and must result from experience.
Ecological Theory	Bronfenbrenner's Ecological theory is an environmental system view of development, involving five systems: microsystem, mesosystem, exosystem, macrosystem, and chronosystem. These emphasize the role of social contexts in development.
Ecology	Ecology refers to the branch of biology that deals with the relationships between living organisms and their environment.
Dynamic Systems Theory	Dynamic Systems Theory believes that in order to develop motor skills, infants must perceive something in the environment that motivates them to act, and they must use their perceptions to fine-tune their movements. Motor skills represent solutions to the infant's goals. The behavior is the result of many converging factors.
Affordance	An affordance is a property of an object, or a feature of the immediate environment, that indicates how that object or feature can be interfaced with. The empty space within an open doorway, for instance, affords movement across that threshold.
Cerebral palsy	Cerebral palsy is a group of permanent disorders associated with developmental brain injuries that occur during fetal development, birth, or shortly after birth. It is characterized by a disruption of motor skills, with symptoms such as spasticity, paralysis, or seizures.
Variable	A variable refers to a measurable factor, characteristic, or attribute of an individual or a system.
Population	Population refers to all members of a well-defined group of organisms, events, or things.
Individuality	According to Cooper, individuality consists of two dimensions: self-assertion and separateness.
Ecological psychology	Ecological psychology emphasises real world studies of behavior as opposed to the artificial environment of the laboratory.
Gestalt psychology	According to Gestalt psychology, people naturally organize their perceptions according to certain patterns. The tendency is to organize perceptions into wholes and to integrate

Go to **Cram101.com** for the Practice Tests for this Chapter.

separate stimuli into meaningful patterns.

Roger Barker	In his classic work "Ecological Psychology" (1968), Roger Barker argued that human behavior was radically situated: in other words, you couldn't make predictions about human behavior unless you know what situation or context or environment the human in question was in.
Lewin	Lewin ranks as one of the pioneers of social psychology, as one of the founders of group dynamics and as one of the most eminent representatives of Gestalt psychology.
Life space	Life space, according to Lewin, is the sum total of the psychological facts of an individual.
Shaping	The concept of reinforcing successive, increasingly accurate approximations to a target behavior is called shaping. The target behavior is broken down into a hierarchy of elemental steps, each step more sophisticated then the last. By successively reinforcing each of the the elemental steps, a form of differential reinforcement, until that step is learned while extinguishing the step below, the target behavior is gradually achieved.
Bronfenbrenner	Bronfenbrenner was a co-founder of the U.S. national Head Start program and founder of the Ecological Theory of Development.
Accommodation	Piaget's developmental process of accommodation is the modification of currently held schemes or new schemes so that new information inconsistent with the existing schemes can be integrated and understood.
Premise	A premise is a statement presumed true within the context of a discourse, especially of a logical argument.
Chronosystem	A chronosystem refers to the patterning of environmental events and transitions over the life course and their sociohistorical contexts.
Microsystem	The setting or context in which an individual lives, including the person's family, peers, school, and neighborhood is a microsystem.
Mesosystem	Relationships between microsystems or connections between contexts, such as the connection between family experience and the school experience are referred to as a mesosystem.
Exosystem	The level at which experiences in another social setting, in which the individual does not have an active role, influence what the individual experiences in an immediate context is referred to as the exosystem.
Perception	Perception is the process of acquiring, interpreting, selecting, and organizing sensory information.
Attitude	An enduring mental representation of a person, place, or thing that evokes an emotional response and related behavior is called attitude.
Affect	A subjective feeling or emotional tone often accompanied by bodily expressions noticeable to others is called affect.
Trust versus mistrust	In Erikson's first stage of psychosexual development, trust versus mistrust, children do-or do not-come to trust that primary caregivers and the environment will meet their needs. The first year of life is the key time for the development of attachment.
Autonomy	Autonomy is the condition of something that does not depend on anything else.
Toddler	A toddler is a child between the ages of one and three years old. During this period, the child learns a great deal about social roles and develops motor skills; to toddle is to walk unsteadily.
Anxiety	Anxiety is a complex combination of the feeling of fear, apprehension and worry often accompanied by physical sensations such as palpitations, chest pain and/or shortness of breath.

Guilt	Guilt describes many concepts related to a negative emotion or condition caused by actions which are believed to be, morally wrong. According to Freud, the avoidance of guilt is the basis for moral behavior.
Puberty	Puberty refers to the process of physical changes by which a child's body becomes an adult body capable of reproduction.
Generativity	Generativity refers to an adult's concern for and commitment to the well-being of future generations.
Wisdom	Wisdom is the ability to make correct judgments and decisions. It is an intangible quality gained through experience. Whether or not something is wise is determined in a pragmatic sense by its popularity, how long it has been around, and its ability to predict against future events.
Cognition	The intellectual processes through which information is obtained, transformed, stored, retrieved, and otherwise used is cognition.
Insight	Insight refers to a sudden awareness of the relationships among various elements that had previously appeared to be independent of one another.
Adaptation	Adaptation is a lowering of sensitivity to a stimulus following prolonged exposure to that stimulus. Behavioral adaptations are special ways a particular organism behaves to survive in its natural habitat.
Assimilation	According to Piaget, assimilation is the process of the organism interacting with the environment given the organism's cognitive structure. Assimilation is reuse of schemas to fit new information.
Prenatal	Prenatal period refers to the time from conception to birth.
Habit	A habit is a response that has become completely separated from its eliciting stimulus. Early learning theorists used the term to describe S-R associations, however not all S-R associations become a habit, rather many are extinguished after reinforcement is withdrawn.
Primary circular reaction	A primary circular reaction is a scheme based on the attempt to reproduce an event that initially occurred by chance.
Stimulus	A change in an environmental condition that elicits a response is a stimulus.
Secondary Circular Reactions	The third stage of Piaget's sensorimotor substages, Secondary Circular Reactions, occurs from four to nine months. The critical requirement for the infant to progress into this substage is hand-eye coordination. Three novelties occur at this stage: intentional grasping for a desired object, repetition of an action involving an external object, and differentiations between ends and means.
Schema	Schema refers to a way of mentally representing the world, such as a belief or an expectation, that can influence perception of persons, objects, and situations.
Schemata	Cognitive categories or frames of reference are called schemata.
Tertiary Circular Reactions	Stage five of the sensorimotor substages, Tertiary Circular Reactions, lasts from twelve to eighteen months, and involves the discovery of new means to meet goals. Piaget describes the child at this juncture as the "young scientist."
Reasoning	Reasoning is the act of using reason to derive a conclusion from certain premises. There are two main methods to reach a conclusion, deductive reasoning and inductive reasoning.
Mental combinations	In Piaget's theory, the final substage of sensorimotor development is a transition between the action-oriented world of the infant and the symbol-oriented world of the child. The stage

Go to **Cram101.com** for the Practice Tests for this Chapter.

	is characterized by mental combinations.
Reflection	Reflection is the process of rephrasing or repeating thoughts and feelings expressed, making the person more aware of what they are saying or thinking.
Parallel play	Parallel play is playing with similar objects, clearly beside others but not with them. (Near but not with others.)
Object permanence	Object permanence is the term used to describe the awareness that objects continue to exist even when they are no longer visible. According to Piaget, object permance for the infant develops once the sensorimotor stage is complete.
Conservation	Conservation refers to the recognition that basic properties of substances such as weight and mass remain the same even when transformations merely alter their appearance.
Quantitative	A quantitative property is one that exists in a range of magnitudes, and can therefore be measured. Measurements of any particular quantitative property are expressed as as a specific quantity, referred to as a unit, multiplied by a number.
Social role	Social role refers to expected behavior patterns associated with particular social positions.
Reversibility	Reversibility according to Piaget, is recognition that processes can be undone, that things can be made as they were.
Concrete operational	According to Piaget, the period from 7 to 12 years of age, which is characterized by logical thought and a loss of egocentrism, is referred to as concrete operational stage. Conservation skills are formed - understanding that quantity, length or number of items is unrelated to the appearance of the object or items.
Deduction	Deduction refers to reasoning from the general to the particular, as in the case of creating an expected hypothesis for a particular experiment from a general theoretical statement.
Hypothesis	A specific statement about behavior or mental processes that is testable through research is a hypothesis.
Innate	Innate behavior is not learned or influenced by the environment, rather, it is present or predisposed at birth.
Physiological changes	Alterations in heart rate, blood pressure, perspiration, and other involuntary responses are physiological changes.
Affective	Affective is the way people react emotionally, their ability to feel another living thing's pain or joy.
Physical therapy	Physical therapy is a health profession concerned with the assessment, diagnosis, and treatment of disease and disability through physical means. It is based upon principles of medical science, and is generally held to be within the sphere of conventional medicine.

Go to **Cram101.com** for the Practice Tests for this Chapter.

21

Theories	Theories are logically self-consistent models or frameworks describing the behavior of a certain natural or social phenomenon. They are broad explanations and predictions concerning phenomena of interest.
Affective	Affective is the way people react emotionally, their ability to feel another living thing's pain or joy.
Life span	Life span refers to the upper boundary of life, the maximum number of years an individual can live. The maximum life span of human beings is about 120 years of age. Females live an average of 6 years longer than males.
Inference	Inference is the act or process of drawing a conclusion based solely on what one already knows.
Learning	Learning is a relatively permanent change in behavior that results from experience. Thus, to attribute a behavioral change to learning, the change must be relatively permanent and must result from experience.
Encoding	Encoding refers to interpreting; transforming; modifying information so that it can be placed in memory. It is the first stage of information processing.
Decoding	Process of phonetic analysis by which a printed word is converted to spoken form before retrieval from long-term memory is called decoding.
Stages	Stages represent relatively discrete periods of time in which functioning is qualitatively different from functioning at other periods.
Fetus	A fetus develops from the end of the 8th week of pregnancy (when the major structures have formed), until birth.
Reflex	A simple, involuntary response to a stimulus is referred to as reflex. Reflex actions originate at the spinal cord rather than the brain.
Stepping reflex	The stepping reflex is where infants take steps when held under the arms and leaned forward so that the feet press against the ground.
Grasping reflex	The grasping reflex is a neonatal reflex that occurs when something touches the infant's palms. The infant responds by grasping tightly.
Motor cortex	Motor cortex refers to the section of cortex that lies in the frontal lobe, just across the central fissure from the sensory cortex. Neural impulses in the motor cortex are linked to muscular responses throughout the body.
Brain	The brain controls and coordinates most movement, behavior and homeostatic body functions such as heartbeat, blood pressure, fluid balance and body temperature. Functions of the brain are responsible for cognition, emotion, memory, motor learning and other sorts of learning. The brain is primarily made up of two types of cells: glia and neurons.
Cerebral cortex	The cerebral cortex is the outermost layer of the cerebrum and has a grey color. It is made up of four lobes and it is involved in many complex brain functions including memory, perceptual awareness, "thinking", language and consciousness. The cerebral cortex receives sensory information from many different sensory organs eg: eyes, ears, etc. and processes the information.
Sensorimotor	The first of Piaget's stages is the Sensorimotor stage. This stage typically ranges from birth to 2 years. In this stage, children experience the world through their senses. During this stage, object permanence and stranger anxiety develop.
Attention	Attention is the cognitive process of selectively concentrating on one thing while ignoring other things. Psychologists have labeled three types of attention: sustained attention, selective attention, and divided attention.

Acquisition	Acquisition is the process of adapting to the environment, learning or becoming conditioned. In classical conditoning terms, it is the initial learning of the stimulus response link, which involves a neutral stimulus being associated with a unconditioned stimulus and becoming a conditioned stimulus.
Variable	A variable refers to a measurable factor, characteristic, or attribute of an individual or a system.
Early childhood	Early childhood refers to the developmental period extending from the end of infancy to about 5 or 6 years of age; sometimes called the preschool years.
Infancy	The developmental period that extends from birth to 18 or 24 months is called infancy.
Child development	Scientific study of the processes of change from conception through adolescence is called child development.
Maturation	The orderly unfolding of traits, as regulated by the genetic code is called maturation.
Ecology	Ecology refers to the branch of biology that deals with the relationships between living organisms and their environment.
Peer pressure	Peer pressure comprises a set of group dynamics whereby a group of people in which one feels comfortable may override the sexual personal habits, individual moral inhibitions or idiosyncratic desires to impose a group norm of attitudes or behaviors.
Reaction time	The amount of time required to respond to a stimulus is referred to as reaction time.
Quantitative	A quantitative property is one that exists in a range of magnitudes, and can therefore be measured. Measurements of any particular quantitative property are expressed as as a specific quantity, referred to as a unit, multiplied by a number.
Affect	A subjective feeling or emotional tone often accompanied by bodily expressions noticeable to others is called affect.
Motivation	In psychology, motivation is the driving force (desire) behind all actions of an organism.
Society	The social sciences use the term society to mean a group of people that form a semi-closed (or semi-open) social system, in which most interactions are with other individuals belonging to the group.
Heuristic	A heuristic is a simple, efficient rule of thumb proposed to explain how people make decisions, come to judgments and solve problems, typically when facing complex problems or incomplete information. These rules work well under most circumstances, but in certain cases lead to systematic cognitive biases.
Algorithm	A systematic procedure for solving a problem that works invariably when it is correctly applied is called an algorithm.
Heredity	Heredity is the transfer of characteristics from parent to offspring through their genes.
Affordance	An affordance is a property of an object, or a feature of the immediate environment, that indicates how that object or feature can be interfaced with. The empty space within an open doorway, for instance, affords movement across that threshold.
Adolescence	The period of life bounded by puberty and the assumption of adult responsibilities is adolescence.
Elaboration	The extensiveness of processing at any given level of memory is called elaboration. The use of elaboration changes developmentally. Adolescents are more likely to use elaboration spontaneously than children.
Physical therapy	Physical therapy is a health profession concerned with the assessment, diagnosis, and

treatment of disease and disability through physical means. It is based upon principles of medical science, and is generally held to be within the sphere of conventional medicine.

Heredity	Heredity is the transfer of characteristics from parent to offspring through their genes.
Individuality	According to Cooper, individuality consists of two dimensions: self-assertion and separateness.
Nervous system	The body's electrochemical communication circuitry, made up of billions of neurons is a nervous system.
Cephalocaudal	The sequence in which the greatest growth occurs at the top, the head, with physical growth in size, weight, and feature differentiation gradually working from top to bottom is referred to as a cephalocaudal pattern.
Proximodistal	Development originating from the center of the body towards the extremities is referred to as proximodistal development. The human embryo normally develops in this fashion and averages 5-10 pounds in brith-weight and between 18 to 22 inches in length.
Infancy	The developmental period that extends from birth to 18 or 24 months is called infancy.
Maturation	The orderly unfolding of traits, as regulated by the genetic code is called maturation.
Postnatal	Postnatal is the period beginning immediately after the birth of a child and extending for about six weeks. The period is also known as postpartum and, less commonly, puerperium.
Prenatal	Prenatal period refers to the time from conception to birth.
Stages	Stages represent relatively discrete periods of time in which functioning is qualitatively different from functioning at other periods.
Fetus	A fetus develops from the end of the 8th week of pregnancy (when the major structures have formed), until birth.
Acquisition	Acquisition is the process of adapting to the environment, learning or becoming conditioned. In classical conditoning terms, it is the initial learning of the stimulus response link, which involves a neutral stimulus being associated with a unconditioned stimulus and becoming a conditioned stimulus.
Regression	Return to a form of behavior characteristic of an earlier stage of development is called regression.
Self-Regulatory	Bandura proposes that self-regulatory systems mediate external influences and provide a basis for purposeful action, allowing people to have personal control over their own thoughts, feelings, motivations, and actions.
Low birth weight	Low birth weight is a fetus that weighs less than 2500 g (5 lb 8 oz) regardless of gestational age.
Plasticity	The capacity for modification and change is referred to as plasticity.
Deprivation	Deprivation, is the loss or withholding of normal stimulation, nutrition, comfort, love, and so forth; a condition of lacking. The level of stimulation is less than what is required.
Attitude	An enduring mental representation of a person, place, or thing that evokes an emotional response and related behavior is called attitude.
Thorndike	Thorndike worked in animal behavior and the learning process leading to the theory of connectionism. Among his most famous contributions were his research on cats escaping from puzzle boxes, and his formulation of the Law of Effect.
Learning	Learning is a relatively permanent change in behavior that results from experience. Thus, to attribute a behavioral change to learning, the change must be relatively permanent and must result from experience.
Motivation	In psychology, motivation is the driving force (desire) behind all actions of an organism.

Go to **Cram101.com** for the Practice Tests for this Chapter.

Attention	Attention is the cognitive process of selectively concentrating on one thing while ignoring other things. Psychologists have labeled three types of attention: sustained attention, selective attention, and divided attention.
Self-esteem	Self-esteem refers to a person's subjective appraisal of himself or herself as intrinsically positive or negative to some degree.
Cognitive skills	Cognitive skills such as reasoning, attention, and memory can be advanced and sustained through practice and training.
Bruner	Bruner has had an enormous impact on educational psychology with his contributions to cognitive learning theory. His ideas are based on categorization, maintaining that people interpret the world in terms of its similarities and differences.
Critical period	A period of time when an innate response can be elicited by a particular stimulus is referred to as the critical period.
Hypothesis	A specific statement about behavior or mental processes that is testable through research is a hypothesis.
Premise	A premise is a statement presumed true within the context of a discourse, especially of a logical argument.
Sensitive period	A sensitive period is a developmental window in which a predisposed behavior is most likely to develop given appropriate stimulation. In linguistic theory, the period from about 18 months to puberty is when the brain is thought to be primed for learning language because of plasticity of the brain.
Individual differences	Individual differences psychology studies the ways in which individual people differ in their behavior. This is distinguished from other aspects of psychology in that although psychology is ostensibly a study of individuals, modern psychologists invariably study groups.
Brain	The brain controls and coordinates most movement, behavior and homeostatic body functions such as heartbeat, blood pressure, fluid balance and body temperature. Functions of the brain are responsible for cognition, emotion, memory, motor learning and other sorts of learning. The brain is primarily made up of two types of cells: glia and neurons.
Variable	A variable refers to a measurable factor, characteristic, or attribute of an individual or a system.
Society	The social sciences use the term society to mean a group of people that form a semi-closed (or semi-open) social system, in which most interactions are with other individuals belonging to the group.
Ontogenetic	The study of the origin and development of an organism is called ontogenetic.
Imprinting	Imprinting describes any kind of critical period sensitive learning (learning occurring at a particular age or a particular life stage) that is rapid and apparently independent of the consequences of behavior.
Attachment	Attachment is the tendency to seek closeness to another person and feel secure when that person is present.
Lorenz	Lorenz demonstrated how incubator-hatched geese would imprint on the first suitable moving stimulus they saw within what he called a "critical period" of about 36 hours shortly after hatching. Most famously, the goslings would imprint on Lorenz himself .
Validity	The extent to which a test measures what it is intended to measure is called validity.
Nature versus nurture	Nature versus nurture is a shorthand expression for debates about the relative importance of an individual's innate makeup versus personal experiences in determining or causing physical

Go to **Cram101.com** for the Practice Tests for this Chapter.

	and behavioral traits.
Identical twins	Identical twins occur when a single egg is fertilized to form one zygote (monozygotic) but the zygote then divides into two separate embryos. The two embryos develop into foetuses sharing the same womb. Monozygotic twins are genetically identical unless there has been a mutation in development, and they are almost always the same gender.
Hilgard	Hilgard made headlines as a pioneer in the scientific study of hypnosis. He and his wife, Josephine, established the Laboratory of Hypnosis Research at Stanford.
Preterm	Born at or prior to completion of 37 weeks of gestation is referred to as preterm.
Toddler	A toddler is a child between the ages of one and three years old. During this period, the child learns a great deal about social roles and develops motor skills; to toddle is to walk unsteadily.
Affect	A subjective feeling or emotional tone often accompanied by bodily expressions noticeable to others is called affect.
Social class	Social class describes the relationships between people in hierarchical societies or cultures. Those with more power usually subordinate those with less power.
Adolescence	The period of life bounded by puberty and the assumption of adult responsibilities is adolescence.
Physiological changes	Alterations in heart rate, blood pressure, perspiration, and other involuntary responses are physiological changes.
Eating disorders	Psychological disorders characterized by distortion of the body image and gross disturbances in eating patterns are called eating disorders.
Gestation period	Gestation period refers to the length of time, normally nine months in human beings, during which a fertilized egg develops into an infant ready to be born.
Mental retardation	Mental retardation refers to having significantly below-average intellectual functioning and limitations in at least two areas of adaptive functioning. Many categorize retardation as mild, moderate, severe, or profound.
Hyperactivity	Hyperactivity can be described as a state in which a individual is abnormally easily excitable and exuberant. Strong emotional reactions and a very short span of attention is also typical for the individual.
Standard deviation	In probability and statistics, the standard deviation is the most commonly used measure of statistical dispersion. Simply put, it measures how spread out the values in a data set are.
Prognosis	A forecast about the probable course of an illess is referred to as prognosis.
Preterm infant	An infant born before completing the thirty-seventh week of gestation is a preterm infant.
Infant mortality	Infant mortality is the death of infants in the first year of life. The leading causes of infant mortality are dehydration and disease. Major causes of infant mortality in more developed countries include congenital malformation, infection and SIDS. Infant mortality rate is the number of newborns dying under a year of age divided by the number of live births during the year.
Statistics	Statistics is a type of data analysis which practice includes the planning, summarizing, and interpreting of observations of a system possibly followed by predicting or forecasting of future events based on a mathematical model of the system being observed.
Congenital	A condition existing at birth is referred to as congenital.
Statistic	A statistic is an observable random variable of a sample.

Obesity	The state of being more than 20 percent above the average weight for a person of one's height is called obesity.
Anorexia	Anorexia nervosa is an eating disorder characterized by voluntary starvation and exercise stress.
Bulimia	Bulimia refers to a disorder in which a person binges on incredibly large quantities of food, then purges by vomiting or by using laxatives. Bulimia is often less about food, and more to do with deep psychological issues and profound feelings of lack of control.
Late adolescence	Late adolescence refers to approximately the latter half of the second decade of life. Career interests, dating, and identity exploration are often more pronounced in late adolescence than in early adolescence.
Cholesterol	Cholesterol is a steroid, a lipid, and an alcohol, found in the cell membranes of all body tissues, and transported in the blood plasma of all animals. Cholesterol is an important component of the membranes of cells, providing stability; it makes the membrane's fluidity stable over a bigger temperature interval.
Glucose	Glucose, a simple monosaccharide sugar, is one of the most important carbohydrates and is used as a source of energy in animals and plants. Glucose is one of the main products of photosynthesis and starts respiration.
Self-image	A person's self-image is the mental picture, generally of a kind that is quite resistant to change, that depicts not only details that are potentially available to objective investigation by others, but also items that have been learned by that person about himself or herself.
Habit	A habit is a response that has become completely separated from its eliciting stimulus. Early learning theorists used the term to describe S-R associations, however not all S-R associations become a habit, rather many are extinguished after reinforcement is withdrawn.
Diabetes	Diabetes is a medical disorder characterized by varying or persistent elevated blood sugar levels, especially after eating. All types of diabetes share similar symptoms and complications at advanced stages: dehydration and ketoacidosis, cardiovascular disease, chronic renal failure, retinal damage which can lead to blindness, nerve damage which can lead to erectile dysfunction, gangrene with risk of amputation of toes, feet, and even legs.
Etiology	Etiology is the study of causation. The term is used in philosophy, physics and biology in reference to the causes of various phenomena. It is generally the study of why things occur, or even the reasons behind the way that things act.
Variability	Statistically, variability refers to how much the scores in a distribution spread out, away from the mean.
Binge eating disorder	Binge eating disorder is a syndrome in which people feel their eating is out of control; eat what most would think is an unusually large amount of food; eat much more quickly than usual; eat until so full they are uncomfortable; eat large amounts of food, even when they are not really hungry; eat alone because they are embarrassed about the amount of food they eat; feel disgusted, depressed, or guilty after overeating.
Population	Population refers to all members of a well-defined group of organisms, events, or things.
Depression	In everyday language depression refers to any downturn in mood, which may be relatively transitory and perhaps due to something trivial. This is differentiated from Clinical depression which is marked by symptoms that last two weeks or more and are so severe that they interfere with daily living.
Binge	Binge refers to relatively brief episode of uncontrolled, excessive consumption.

Anxiety	Anxiety is a complex combination of the feeling of fear, apprehension and worry often accompanied by physical sensations such as palpitations, chest pain and/or shortness of breath.
Emotion	An emotion is a mental states that arise spontaneously, rather than through conscious effort. They are often accompanied by physiological changes.
Osteoporosis	Osteoporosis refers to a disorder of aging that involves an extensive loss of bone tissue and is the main reason many older adults walk with a marked stoop. Women are especially vulnerable to osteoporosis.
Amenorrhea	Amenorrhea (AmE) is the absence of a menstrual period in a woman of reproductive age. Physiologic states of amenorrhea are seen during pregnancy and lactation (breastfeeding). Outside of the reproductive years there is absence of menses during childhood and after menopause.
Psychotherapy	Psychotherapy is a set of techniques based on psychological principles intended to improve mental health, emotional or behavioral issues.
Antidepressant	An antidepressant is a medication used primarily in the treatment of clinical depression. They are not thought to produce tolerance, although sudden withdrawal may produce adverse effects. They create little if any immediate change in mood and require between several days and several weeks to take effect.
Genetics	Genetics is the science of genes, heredity, and the variation of organisms.
Affective	Affective is the way people react emotionally, their ability to feel another living thing's pain or joy.
Child development	Scientific study of the processes of change from conception through adolescence is called child development.
Physical therapy	Physical therapy is a health profession concerned with the assessment, diagnosis, and treatment of disease and disability through physical means. It is based upon principles of medical science, and is generally held to be within the sphere of conventional medicine.
Insight	Insight refers to a sudden awareness of the relationships among various elements that had previously appeared to be independent of one another.
Early Intervention	Early intervention is a process used to recognize warning signs for mental health problems and to take early action against factors that put individuals at risk.

Go to **Cram101.com** for the Practice Tests for this Chapter.

Infant mortality	Infant mortality is the death of infants in the first year of life. The leading causes of infant mortality are dehydration and disease. Major causes of infant mortality in more developed countries include congenital malformation, infection and SIDS. Infant mortality rate is the number of newborns dying under a year of age divided by the number of live births during the year.
Prenatal	Prenatal period refers to the time from conception to birth.
Society	The social sciences use the term society to mean a group of people that form a semi-closed (or semi-open) social system, in which most interactions are with other individuals belonging to the group.
Population	Population refers to all members of a well-defined group of organisms, events, or things.
Perinatal	Perinatal is the period occurring around the time of birth (5 months before and 1 month after).
Affect	A subjective feeling or emotional tone often accompanied by bodily expressions noticeable to others is called affect.
Postnatal	Postnatal is the period beginning immediately after the birth of a child and extending for about six weeks. The period is also known as postpartum and, less commonly, puerperium.
Teratogenic	Capacity for causing birth defects is referred to as teratogenic.
Fetus	A fetus develops from the end of the 8th week of pregnancy (when the major structures have formed), until birth.
Teratogen	Teratogen refers to from the Greek word tera, meaning 'monster.' It is any agent that causes a birth defect.
Malnutrition	Malnutrition is a general term for the medical condition in a person or animal caused by an unbalanced diet—either too little or too much food, or a diet missing one or more important nutrients.
Syndrome	The term syndrome is the association of several clinically recognizable features, signs, symptoms, phenomena or characteristics which often occur together, so that the presence of one feature indicates the presence of the others.
Placenta	A membrane that permits the exchange of nutrients and waste products between the mother and her developing child but does not allow the maternal and fetal bloodstreams to mix is the placenta.
Statistics	Statistics is a type of data analysis which practice includes the planning, summarizing, and interpreting of observations of a system possibly followed by predicting or forecasting of future events based on a mathematical model of the system being observed.
Statistic	A statistic is an observable random variable of a sample.
Hypoxia	Hypoxia is a pathological condition in which the body as a whole or region of the body is deprived of adequate oxygen supply.
Umbilical cord	The umbilical cord is a tube that connects a developing embryo or fetus to its placenta. It contains major arteries and veins for the exchange of nutrient- and oxygen-rich blood between the embryo and placenta.
Infancy	The developmental period that extends from birth to 18 or 24 months is called infancy.
Child development	Scientific study of the processes of change from conception through adolescence is called child development.
Socioeconomic	Socioeconomic pertains to the study of the social and economic impacts of any product or

Go to **Cram101.com** for the Practice Tests for this Chapter.
And, **NEVER** highlight a book again!

	service offering, market intervention or other activity on an economy as a whole and on the companies, organization and individuals who are its main economic actors.
Anxiety	Anxiety is a complex combination of the feeling of fear, apprehension and worry often accompanied by physical sensations such as palpitations, chest pain and/or shortness of breath.
Trauma	Trauma refers to a severe physical injury or wound to the body caused by an external force, or a psychological shock having a lasting effect on mental life.
Habit	A habit is a response that has become completely separated from its eliciting stimulus. Early learning theorists used the term to describe S-R associations, however not all S-R associations become a habit, rather many are extinguished after reinforcement is withdrawn.
Low birth weight	Low birth weight is a fetus that weighs less than 2500 g (5 lb 8 oz) regardless of gestational age.
Spina bifida	Spina bifida are birth defects caused by an incomplete closure of one or more vertebral arches of the spine, resulting in malformations of the spinal cord. Spina bifida results in varying degrees of paralysis, absence of skin sensation, incontinence, and spine and limb problems depending on the severity and location of the lesion damage on the spine.
Neural tube	The neural tube is the embryonal structure that gives rise to the brain and spinal cord.
Preterm	Born at or prior to completion of 37 weeks of gestation is referred to as preterm.
Predisposition	Predisposition refers to an inclination or diathesis to respond in a certain way, either inborn or acquired. In abnormal psychology, it is a factor that lowers the ability to withstand stress and inclines the individual toward pathology.
Socioeconomic Status	A family's socioeconomic status is based on family income, parental education level, parental occupation, and social status in the community. Those with high status often have more success in preparing their children for school because they have access to a wide range of resources.
Liver	The liver plays a major role in metabolism and has a number of functions in the body including detoxification, glycogen storage and plasma protein synthesis. It also produces bile, which is important for digestion. The liver converts most carbohydrates, proteing, and fats into glucose.
Toxemia	Toxemia is another term for blood poisoning, or the presence in the bloodstream of quantities of bacteria or bacterial toxins sufficient to cause serious illness.
Brain	The brain controls and coordinates most movement, behavior and homeostatic body functions such as heartbeat, blood pressure, fluid balance and body temperature. Functions of the brain are responsible for cognition, emotion, memory, motor learning and other sorts of learning. The brain is primarily made up of two types of cells: glia and neurons.
Epilepsy	Epilepsy is a chronic neurological condition characterized by recurrent unprovoked neural discharges. It is commonly controlled with medication, although surgical methods are used as well.
Seizure	A seizure is a temporary alteration in brain function expressed as a changed mental state, tonic or clonic movements and various other symptoms. They are due to temporary abnormal electrical activity of a group of brain cells.
Chemotherapy	Chemotherapy is the use of chemical substances to treat disease. In its modern-day use, it refers almost exclusively to cytostatic drugs used to treat cancer.In its non-oncological use, the term may also refer to antibiotics.
Progesterone	A female sex hormone that promotes growth of the sex organs and helps maintain pregnancy is

	called progesterone.
Thalidomide	Thalidomide is a drug which was sold during the 1950s and 1960s as a sleeping aid and to pregnant women as an antiemetic to combat morning sickness and other symptoms. It was later (1960–61) found to be teratogenic in fetal development, most visibly as a cause of amelia or phocomelia.
Sedative	A sedative is a drug that depresses the central nervous system (CNS), which causes calmness, relaxation, reduction of anxiety, sleepiness, slowed breathing, slurred speech, staggering gait, poor judgment, and slow, uncertain reflexes.
Diabetes	Diabetes is a medical disorder characterized by varying or persistent elevated blood sugar levels, especially after eating. All types of diabetes share similar symptoms and complications at advanced stages: dehydration and ketoacidosis, cardiovascular disease, chronic renal failure, retinal damage which can lead to blindness, nerve damage which can lead to erectile dysfunction, gangrene with risk of amputation of toes, feet, and even legs.
Spinal cord	The spinal cord is a part of the vertebrate nervous system that is enclosed in and protected by the vertebral column (it passes through the spinal canal). It consists of nerve cells. The spinal cord carries sensory signals and motor innervation to most of the skeletal muscles in the body.
Lysergic acid	Lysergic acid is a precursor for a wide range of ergoline alkaloids that are produced by the ergot fungus and some plants. Amides of lysergic acid, commonly called lysergamides, are widely used as pharmaceuticals and as hallucinogenic drugs (LSD).
Amphetamine	Amphetamine is a synthetic stimulant used to suppress the appetite, control weight, and treat disorders including narcolepsy and ADHD. It is also used recreationally and for performance enhancement.
Marijuana	Marijuana is the dried vegetable matter of the Cannabis sativa plant. It contains large concentrations of compounds that have medicinal and psychoactive effects when consumed, usually by smoking or eating.
Cannabis	The hemp plant from which marijuana, hashish, and THC are derived is the cannabis.
Hashish	Hashish is a psychoactive drug derived from the Cannabis plant. It is used for its relaxing and mind-altering effects.
Opiates	A group of narcotics derived from the opium poppy that provide a euphoric rush and depress the nervous system are referred to as opiates.
Heroin	Heroin is widely and illegally used as a powerful and addictive drug producing intense euphoria, which often disappears with increasing tolerance. Heroin is a semi-synthetic opioid. It is the 3,6-diacetyl derivative of morphine and is synthesised from it by acetylation.
Opium	Opium is a narcotic analgesic drug which is obtained from the unripe seed pods of the opium poppy. Regular use, even for a few days, invariably leads to physical tolerance and dependence. Various degrees of psychological addiction can occur, though this is relatively rare when opioids are properly used..
Attention	Attention is the cognitive process of selectively concentrating on one thing while ignoring other things. Psychologists have labeled three types of attention: sustained attention, selective attention, and divided attention.
Cocaine	Cocaine is a crystalline tropane alkaloid that is obtained from the leaves of the coca plant. It is a stimulant of the central nervous system and an appetite suppressant, creating what has been described as a euphoric sense of happiness and increased energy.

Go to **Cram101.com** for the Practice Tests for this Chapter.

Withdrawal symptoms	Withdrawal symptoms are physiological changes that occur when the use of a drug is stopped or dosage decreased.
Congenital	A condition existing at birth is referred to as congenital.
Alcoholic	An alcoholic is dependent on alcohol as characterized by craving, loss of control, physical dependence and withdrawal symptoms, and tolerance.
Alcoholism	A disorder that involves long-term, repeated, uncontrolled, compulsive, and excessive use of alcoholic beverages and that impairs the drinker's health and work and social relationships is called alcoholism.
Sullivan	Sullivan developed the Self System, a configuration of the personality traits developed in childhood and reinforced by positive affirmation and the security operations developed in childhood to avoid anxiety and threats to self-esteem.
Chronic	Chronic refers to a relatively long duration, usually more than a few months.
Fetal alcohol syndrome	A cluster of abnormalities that appears in the offspring of mothers who drink alcohol heavily during pregnancy is called fetal alcohol syndrome.
Critical period	A period of time when an innate response can be elicited by a particular stimulus is referred to as the critical period.
Sudden infant death syndrome	Sudden Infant Death Syndrome is the term for the sudden and unexplained death of an apparently healthy infant aged one month to one year.
Mental retardation	Mental retardation refers to having significantly below-average intellectual functioning and limitations in at least two areas of adaptive functioning. Many categorize retardation as mild, moderate, severe, or profound.
Asthma	Asthma is a complex disease characterized by bronchial hyperresponsiveness (BHR), inflammation, mucus production and intermittent airway obstruction.
Genetics	Genetics is the science of genes, heredity, and the variation of organisms.
Heredity	Heredity is the transfer of characteristics from parent to offspring through their genes.
Human genome project	The Human Genome Project (HGP) endeavored to map the human genome down to the nucleotide (or base pair) level and to identify all the genes present in it.
Chromosome	The DNA which carries genetic information in biological cells is normally packaged in the form of one or more large macromolecules called a chromosome. Humans normally have 46.
Mitosis	Mitosis is the process by which a cell separates its duplicated genome into two identical halves.
Embryo	A developed zygote that has a rudimentary heart, brain, and other organs is referred to as an embryo.
Gene	A gene is an ultramicroscopic area of the chromosome. It is the smallest physical unit of the DNA molecule that carries a piece of hereditary information.
Spontaneous abortion	Spontaneous abortion is the natural or accidental termination of a pregnancy at a stage where the embryo or the fetus is incapable of surviving, generally defined at a gestation less than 20 weeks.
Down syndrome	Down syndrome encompasses a number of genetic disorders, of which trisomy 21 (a nondisjunction, the so-called extrachromosone) is the most representative, causing highly variable degrees of learning difficulties as well as physical disabilities. Incidence of Down syndrome is estimated at 1 per 660 births, making it the most common chromosomal abnormality.
Trisomy	A condition wherein there are three rather than the usual pair of homologous chromosomes

within the cell nucleus is referred to as trisomy.

Acquisition	Acquisition is the process of adapting to the environment, learning or becoming conditioned. In classical conditoning terms, it is the initial learning of the stimulus response link, which involves a neutral stimulus being associated with a unconditioned stimulus and becoming a conditioned stimulus.
Mutation	Mutation is a permanent, sometimes transmissible (if the change is to a germ cell) change to the genetic material (usually DNA or RNA) of a cell. They can be caused by copying errors in the genetic material during cell division and by exposure to radiation, chemicals, or viruses, or can occur deliberately under cellular control during the processes such as meiosis or hypermutation.
Tay-Sachs disease	Tay-Sachs disease is a fatal genetic disorder, inherited in an autosomal recessive pattern, in which harmful quantities of a fatty substance called ganglioside GM2 accumulate in the nerve cells in the brain.
Phenylketonuria	Phenylketonuria is a genetic disorder in which an individual cannot properly metabolize amino acids. The disorder is now easily detected but, if left untreated, results in mental retardation and hyperactivity.
Early adulthood	The developmental period beginning in the late teens or early twenties and lasting into the thirties is called early adulthood; characterized by an increasing self-awareness.
Trait	An enduring personality characteristic that tends to lead to certain behaviors is called a trait. The term trait also means a genetically inherited feature of an organism.
Amniocentesis	Amniocentesis is a medical procedure used for prenatal diagnosis, in which from the amnion around a developing fetus a small amount of amniotic fluid is extracted. It is usually offered when there may be an increased risk for genetic conditions in the pregnancy.
Metabolic disorder	A metabolic disorder is a medical disorder which affects the production of energy within individual human (or animal) cells. Most metabolic disorders are genetic, though a few are "acquired" as a result of diet, toxins, infections, etc.
Recessive gene	Recessive gene refers to an allele that causes a phenotype (visible or detectable characteristic) that is only seen in a homozygous genotype (an organism that has two copies of the same allele). Thus, both parents have to be carriers of a recessive trait in order for a child to express that trait.
Phenylalanine	Phenylalanine is an essential amino acid. The genetic disorder phenylketonuria is an inability to metabolize phenylalanine.
Amino acid	Amino acid is the basic structural building unit of proteins. They form short polymer chains called peptides or polypeptides which in turn form structures called proteins.
Tyrosine	Tyrosine is one of the 20 amino acids that are used by cells to synthesize proteins. It plays a key role in signal transduction, since it can be tagged (phosphorylated) with a phosphate group by protein kinases to alter the functionality and activity of certain enzymes.
Enzyme	An enzyme is a protein that catalyzes, or speeds up, a chemical reaction. Enzymes are essential to sustain life because most chemical reactions in biological cells would occur too slowly, or would lead to different products, without enzymes.
Severe mental retardation	A limitation in mental development as measured on the Wechsler Adult Intelligence Scale with scores between 20 -34 is called severe mental retardation.
Iris	The iris is the most visible part of the eye. The iris is an annulus (or flattened ring) consisting of pigmented fibrovascular tissue known as a stroma. The stroma connects a sphincter muscle, which contracts the pupil, and a set of dialator muscles which open it.

Sensation	Sensation is the first stage in the chain of biochemical and neurologic events that begins with the impinging of a stimulus upon the receptor cells of a sensory organ, which then leads to perception, the mental state that is reflected in statements like "I see a uniformly blue wall."
Ultrasound	Ultrasound is sound with a frequency greater than the upper limit of human hearing, approximately 20 kilohertz. Medical use can visualise muscle and soft tissue, making them useful for scanning the organs, and obstetric ultrasonography is commonly used during pregnancy.
Variable	A variable refers to a measurable factor, characteristic, or attribute of an individual or a system.
Acquired immunodeficiency syndrome	Acquired Immunodeficiency Syndrome is defined as a collection of symptoms and infections resulting from the depletion of the immune system caused by infection with the human immunodeficiency virus, commonly called HIV.
Sexually Transmitted Disease	Sexually transmitted disease is commonly transmitted between partners through some form of sexual activity, most commonly vaginal intercourse, oral sex, or anal sex.
Genital herpes	Genital herpes refers to a sexually transmitted disease caused by a large family of viruses of different strains. These strains also produce other, nonsexually transmitted diseases such as chicken pox and mononucleosis.
Chlamydia	Chlamydia is currently one of the most common sexually transmitted disease. It can cause genital infections, conjunctivitis, pelvic inflammatory disease, pneumonia, urethritis, Fitz-Hugh-Curtis syndrome, Reiter's syndrome and lymphogranuloma venereum.
Gonorrhea	Gonorrhea is among the most common curable sexually transmitted diseases in the world. In men, epididymitis, prostatitis and urethral stricture can result from untreated gonorrhoea. In women, Bartholinitis and abscess formation, pelvic inflammatory disease and Fitz-Hugh-Curtis syndrome can occur.
Syphilis	Syphilis is a sexually transmitted disease that is caused by a spirochaete bacterium, Treponema pallidum. If not treated, syphilis can cause serious effects such as damage to the nervous system, heart, or brain. Untreated syphilis can be ultimately fatal.
Rubella	An infectious disease that, if contracted by the mother during the first three months of pregnancy, has a high risk of causing mental retardation and physical deformity in the child is called rubella.
Asymptomatic	A disease is asymptomatic when it is at a stage where the patient does not experience symptoms. By their nature, asymptomatic diseases are not usually discovered until the patient undergoes medical tests (X-rays or other investigations). Some diseases remain asymptomatic for a remarkably long time, including some forms of cancer.
Measles	Measles, also known as rubeola, is a common disease caused by a virus of the genus Morbillivirus. Complications with measles are relatively common, ranging from relatively common and less serious diarrhea, to pneumonia and encephalitis. Complications are usually more severe amongst infants and adults who catch the virus.
Cognitive development	The process by which a child's understanding of the world changes as a function of age and experience is called cognitive development.
Fetal period	The prenatal period of development that begins 2 months after conception and lasts for 7 months, on the average is called the fetal period.
Chemical imbalance	Chemical imbalance refers to relative excess or deficit in brain chemicals, such as neurotransmitters, that may be implicated in some psychological disorders.

Hypothyroidism	Hypothyroidism refers to slower metabolism and sluggishness caused by an underactive thyroid gland.
Thyroxine	The thyroid hormones, thyroxine and triiodothyronine (T3), are tyrosine-based hormones produced by the thyroid gland. They act on the body to increase the basal metabolic rate, affect protein synthesis and increase the body's sensitivity to catecholamines (such as adrenaline).
Cretinism	Cretinism is a condition of severely stunted physical and mental growth due to untreated congenital deficiency of thyroid hormones (hypothyroidism).
Thyroid	In anatomy, the thyroid is the largest endocrine gland in the body. The primary function of the thyroid is production of hormones.
Stages	Stages represent relatively discrete periods of time in which functioning is qualitatively different from functioning at other periods.
Rh factor	The two most important classifications to describe blood types in humans are ABO and the Rh factor. If the Rh factor is present in the blood of a fetus but not in that of the mother, her system produces antibodies that may enter the bloodstream of the fetus and indirectly damage the brain.
Nervous system	The body's electrochemical communication circuitry, made up of billions of neurons is a nervous system.
Endocrine system	The endocrine system is a control system of ductless endocrine glands that secrete chemical messengers called hormones that circulate within the body via the bloodstream to affect distant organs. It does not include exocrine glands such as salivary glands, sweat glands and glands within the gastrointestinal tract.
Cerebral cortex	The cerebral cortex is the outermost layer of the cerebrum and has a grey color. It is made up of four lobes and it is involved in many complex brain functions including memory, perceptual awareness, "thinking", language and consciousness. The cerebral cortex receives sensory information from many different sensory organs eg: eyes, ears, etc. and processes the information.
Hypothalamus	The hypothalamus is a region of the brain located below the thalamus, forming the major portion of the ventral region of the diencephalon and functioning to regulate certain metabolic processes and other autonomic activities.
Thalamus	An area near the center of the brain involved in the relay of sensory information to the cortex and in the functions of sleep and attention is the thalamus.
Autonomic nervous system	A division of the peripheral nervous system, the autonomic nervous system, regulates glands and activities such as heartbeat, respiration, digestion, and dilation of the pupils. It is responsible for homeostasis, maintaining a relatively constant internal environment .
Learning	Learning is a relatively permanent change in behavior that results from experience. Thus, to attribute a behavioral change to learning, the change must be relatively permanent and must result from experience.
Amniotic fluid	Amniotic fluid refers to fluid within the amniotic sac that suspends and protects the fetus.
Chorionic villus sampling	Chorionic villus sampling is a form of prenatal diagnosis to determine genetic abnormalities in the fetus. It entails getting a sample of the placental tissue and testing it.
Uterus	The uterus or womb is the major female reproductive organ. The main function of the uterus is to accept a fertilized ovum which becomes implanted into the endometrium, and derives nourishment from blood vessels which develop exclusively for this purpose.
Fetoscopy	Fetoscopy is an endoscopic procedure during pregnancy to allow access to the fetus, the

amniotic cavity, the umbilical cord, and the fetal side of the placenta.

Magnetic resonance imaging	Magnetic resonance imaging is a method of creating images of the inside of opaque organs in living organisms as well as detecting the amount of bound water in geological structures. It is primarily used to demonstrate pathological or other physiological alterations of living tissues and is a commonly used form of medical imaging.
Cervix	The cervix is the lower end of the uterus that joins with the top portion of the vaginia.
Amniotic sac	The amniotic sac is a tough but thin transparent pair of membranes, which hold a developing embryo (and later fetus) until shortly before birth. The inner membrane, the amnion, contains the amniotic fluid and the fetus.
Cesarean section	A cesarean section is a form of childbirth in which a surgical incision is made through a mother's abdomen and uterus to deliver one or more babies. It is usually performed when a vaginal delivery would lead to medical complications.
Anoxia	Asphyxia is a condition of severely deficient supply of oxygen to the body. In the absence of remedial action it will very rapidly lead to unconsciousness and death. Anoxia means the pathological state in which tissues do not get (enough of) oxygen. Problems during childbirth can lead to the newborn experiencing asphyxia.
Cerebral palsy	Cerebral palsy is a group of permanent disorders associated with developmental brain injuries that occur during fetal development, birth, or shortly after birth. It is characterized by a disruption of motor skills, with symptoms such as spasticity, paralysis, or seizures.
Lamaze	Modern Lamaze childbirth classes teach expectant mothers breathing techniques and often other ways to work with the labor process to reduce the pain often associated with childbirth.

Prenatal	Prenatal period refers to the time from conception to birth.
Fetal period	The prenatal period of development that begins 2 months after conception and lasts for 7 months, on the average is called the fetal period.
Infancy	The developmental period that extends from birth to 18 or 24 months is called infancy.
Fetus	A fetus develops from the end of the 8th week of pregnancy (when the major structures have formed), until birth.
Ovum	Ovum is a female sex cell or gamete.
Fallopian tube	A tube through which the eggs travel from the ovaries to the uterus is a fallopian tube.
In vitro	In vitro is an experimental technique where the experiment is performed in a test tube, or generally outside a living organism or cell.
Chromosome	The DNA which carries genetic information in biological cells is normally packaged in the form of one or more large macromolecules called a chromosome. Humans normally have 46.
Zygote	A zygote is a cell that is the result of fertilization. That is, two haploid cells—usually (but not always) a sperm cell from a male and an ovum from a female—merge into a single diploid cell called the zygote.
Trait	An enduring personality characteristic that tends to lead to certain behaviors is called a trait. The term trait also means a genetically inherited feature of an organism.
Germinal period	The germinal period refers to the period of prenatal development that takes place in the first 2 weeks after conception. It includes the creation of the zygote, continued cell division, and the attachment of the zygote to the uterine wall.
Mitosis	Mitosis is the process by which a cell separates its duplicated genome into two identical halves.
Stages	Stages represent relatively discrete periods of time in which functioning is qualitatively different from functioning at other periods.
Uterus	The uterus or womb is the major female reproductive organ. The main function of the uterus is to accept a fertilized ovum which becomes implanted into the endometrium, and derives nourishment from blood vessels which develop exclusively for this purpose.
Ovulation	Ovulation is the process in the menstrual cycle by which a mature ovarian follicle ruptures and discharges an ovum (also known as an oocyte, female gamete, or casually, an egg) that participates in reproduction.
Spontaneous abortion	Spontaneous abortion is the natural or accidental termination of a pregnancy at a stage where the embryo or the fetus is incapable of surviving, generally defined at a gestation less than 20 weeks.
Statistic	A statistic is an observable random variable of a sample.
Embryonic period	Embryonic period refers to the period of prenatal development that occurs 2 to 8 weeks after conception. During the embryonic period, the rate of cell differentiation intensifies, support systems for the cells form, and organs appear.
Embryo	A developed zygote that has a rudimentary heart, brain, and other organs is referred to as an embryo.
Nervous system	The body's electrochemical communication circuitry, made up of billions of neurons is a nervous system.
Ectoderm	Ectoderm refers to the outermost cell layer of the newly formed embryo, from which the skin and nervous systems develop.

Go to **Cram101.com** for the Practice Tests for this Chapter.
And, **NEVER** highlight a book again!

Mesoderm	The mesoderm is one of the three germ layers in the early developing embryo. The mesoderm gives rise to tissues including connective tissue, muscles and the circulatory system.
Placenta	A membrane that permits the exchange of nutrients and waste products between the mother and her developing child but does not allow the maternal and fetal bloodstreams to mix is the placenta.
Umbilical cord	The umbilical cord is a tube that connects a developing embryo or fetus to its placenta. It contains major arteries and veins for the exchange of nutrient- and oxygen-rich blood between the embryo and placenta.
Amnion	The amniotic sac is a tough but thin transparent pair of membranes, which hold a developing embryo (and later fetus) until shortly before birth. The inner membrane, the amnion, contains the amniotic fluid and the fetus.
Congenital	A condition existing at birth is referred to as congenital.
Brain	The brain controls and coordinates most movement, behavior and homeostatic body functions such as heartbeat, blood pressure, fluid balance and body temperature. Functions of the brain are responsible for cognition, emotion, memory, motor learning and other sorts of learning. The brain is primarily made up of two types of cells: glia and neurons.
Reflex	A simple, involuntary response to a stimulus is referred to as reflex. Reflex actions originate at the spinal cord rather than the brain.
Amniotic fluid	Amniotic fluid refers to fluid within the amniotic sac that suspends and protects the fetus.
Amniocentesis	Amniocentesis is a medical procedure used for prenatal diagnosis, in which from the amnion around a developing fetus a small amount of amniotic fluid is extracted. It is usually offered when there may be an increased risk for genetic conditions in the pregnancy.
Lanugo	Lanugo are hairs that grow on the body to attempt to insulate it because of lack of fat. It is normal in gestating fetuses. Lanugo hair is usually shed and replaced by vellus hair at 36-40 weeks gestation. The presence of lanugo in newborns is a sign of premature birth.
Vernix	An oily, white substance that coats the skin of the neonate, especially preterm babies is referred to as vernix.
Gland	A gland is an organ in an animal's body that synthesizes a substance for release such as hormones, often into the bloodstream or into cavities inside the body or its outer surface.
Cephalocaudal	The sequence in which the greatest growth occurs at the top, the head, with physical growth in size, weight, and feature differentiation gradually working from top to bottom is referred to as a cephalocaudal pattern.
Proximodistal	Development originating from the center of the body towards the extremities is referred to as proximodistal development. The human embroyo normally develops in this fashion and averages 5-10 pounds in brith-weight and between 18 to 22 inches in length.
Neonatal period	The first 4 weeks of life, a time of transition from intrauterine dependency to independent existence is called the neonatal period.
Postnatal	Postnatal is the period beginning immediately after the birth of a child and extending for about six weeks. The period is also known as postpartum and, less commonly, puerperium.
Socioeconomic	Socioeconomic pertains to the study of the social and economic impacts of any product or service offering, market intervention or other activity on an economy as a whole and on the companies, organization and individuals who are its main economic actors.
Malnutrition	Malnutrition is a general term for the medical condition in a person or animal caused by an unbalanced diet—either too little or too much food, or a diet missing one or more important

Go to **Cram101.com** for the Practice Tests for this Chapter.

	nutrients.
Normal curve	Normal curve refers to graphic presentation of a normal distribution, which shows a characteristic bell shape.
Population	Population refers to all members of a well-defined group of organisms, events, or things.
Statistics	Statistics is a type of data analysis which practice includes the planning, summarizing, and interpreting of observations of a system possibly followed by predicting or forecasting of future events based on a mathematical model of the system being observed.
Correlation	A statistical technique for determining the degree of association between two or more variables is referred to as correlation.
Acquisition	Acquisition is the process of adapting to the environment, learning or becoming conditioned. In classical conditoning terms, it is the initial learning of the stimulus response link, which involves a neutral stimulus being associated with a unconditioned stimulus and becoming a conditioned stimulus.
Maturation	The orderly unfolding of traits, as regulated by the genetic code is called maturation.
Physiology	The study of the functions and activities of living cells, tissues, and organs and of the physical and chemical phenomena involved is referred to as physiology.
Child development	Scientific study of the processes of change from conception through adolescence is called child development.

Reflex	A simple, involuntary response to a stimulus is referred to as reflex. Reflex actions originate at the spinal cord rather than the brain.
Fetus	A fetus develops from the end of the 8th week of pregnancy (when the major structures have formed), until birth.
Brain	The brain controls and coordinates most movement, behavior and homeostatic body functions such as heartbeat, blood pressure, fluid balance and body temperature. Functions of the brain are responsible for cognition, emotion, memory, motor learning and other sorts of learning. The brain is primarily made up of two types of cells: glia and neurons.
Cerebral cortex	The cerebral cortex is the outermost layer of the cerebrum and has a grey color. It is made up of four lobes and it is involved in many complex brain functions including memory, perceptual awareness, "thinking", language and consciousness. The cerebral cortex receives sensory information from many different sensory organs eg: eyes, ears, etc. and processes the information.
Nerve impulse	A nerve impulse is a change in the electric potential of a neuron; a wave of depolarization spreads along the neuron and causes the release of a neurotransmitter.
Motor neuron	A motor neuron is an efferent neuron that originates in the spinal cord and synapses with muscle fibers to facilitate muscle contraction and with muscle spindles to modify proprioceptive sensitivity.
Nervous system	The body's electrochemical communication circuitry, made up of billions of neurons is a nervous system.
Insight	Insight refers to a sudden awareness of the relationships among various elements that had previously appeared to be independent of one another.
Tactile	Pertaining to the sense of touch is referred to as tactile.
Sensorimotor	The first of Piaget's stages is the Sensorimotor stage. This stage typically ranges from birth to 2 years. In this stage, children experience the world through their senses. During this stage, object permanence and stranger anxiety develop.
Neonatal period	The first 4 weeks of life, a time of transition from intrauterine dependency to independent existence is called the neonatal period.
Infancy	The developmental period that extends from birth to 18 or 24 months is called infancy.
Neurologist	A physician who studies the nervous system, especially its structure, functions, and abnormalities is referred to as neurologist.
Hypothesis	A specific statement about behavior or mental processes that is testable through research is a hypothesis.
Dynamic Systems Theory	Dynamic Systems Theory believes that in order to develop motor skills, infants must perceive something in the environment that motivates them to act, and they must use their perceptions to fine-tune their movements. Motor skills represent solutions to the infant's goals. The behavior is the result of many converging factors.
Theories	Theories are logically self-consistent models or frameworks describing the behavior of a certain natural or social phenomenon. They are broad explanations and predictions concerning phenomena of interest.
Sensory neuron	A sensory neuron is an afferent nerve cell within the nervous system responsible for converting external stimuli from the organism's environment into internal electrical impulses. It carries messages from a sensory organ, through a nerve, into the brain or spinal cord.

Myelin	Myelin is an electrically insulating fatty layer that surrounds the axons of many neurons, especially those in the peripheral nervous system. The main consequence of a myelin sheath is an increase in the speed at which impulses propagate along the myelinated fiber. The sheath continues to develop throughout childhood.
Central nervous system	The vertebrate central nervous system consists of the brain and spinal cord.
Perseveration	The persistent repetition of words and ideas, often found in schizophrenia is called perseveration.
Maturation	The orderly unfolding of traits, as regulated by the genetic code is called maturation.
Moro reflex	Moro reflex refers to a neonatal startle response that occurs in reaction to a sudden, intense noise or movement. When startled, the newborn arches its back, throws its head back, and flings out its arms and legs. The primary significance of this reflex is in evaluating integration of the central nervous system (CNS).
Stimulus	A change in an environmental condition that elicits a response is a stimulus.
Sucking reflex	The sucking reflex is a newborn's built-in reaction of automatically sucking an object placed in its mouth. The sucking reflex enables the infant to get nourishment before it has associated a nipple with food.
Grasping reflex	The grasping reflex is a neonatal reflex that occurs when something touches the infant's palms. The infant responds by grasping tightly.
Babinski reflex	A reflex in which infants fan their toes when the undersides of their feet are stroked is called the Babinski reflex.
Stroke	A stroke occurs when the blood supply to a part of the brain is suddenly interrupted by occlusion, by hemorrhage, or other causes
Early childhood	Early childhood refers to the developmental period extending from the end of infancy to about 5 or 6 years of age; sometimes called the preschool years.
Labyrinth	The labyrinth is a system of fluid passages in the inner ear, comprising the vestibular system and the auditory system, which provides the sense of balance.
Otolith	The otolith organs (the utricle and the saccule) are structures in the inner ear that are sensitive to gravity and linear acceleration. Because of their orientation in the head, the utricle is sensitive to a change in horizontal movement, and the saccule gives information about vertical acceleration (such as when in an elevator).
Stepping reflex	The stepping reflex is where infants take steps when held under the arms and leaned forward so that the feet press against the ground.
Affect	A subjective feeling or emotional tone often accompanied by bodily expressions noticeable to others is called affect.
Experimental group	Experimental group refers to any group receiving a treatment effect in an experiment.
Control group	A group that does not receive the treatment effect in an experiment is referred to as the control group or sometimes as the comparison group.
Conditioning	Conditioning describes the process by which behaviors can be learned or modified through interaction with the environment.
Down syndrome	Down syndrome encompasses a number of genetic disorders, of which trisomy 21 (a nondisjunction, the so-called extrachromosone) is the most representative, causing highly variable degrees of learning difficulties as well as physical disabilities. Incidence of Down

Go to **Cram101.com** for the Practice Tests for this Chapter.
And, **NEVER** highlight a book again!

	syndrome is estimated at 1 per 660 births, making it the most common chromosomal abnormality.
Learning	Learning is a relatively permanent change in behavior that results from experience. Thus, to attribute a behavioral change to learning, the change must be relatively permanent and must result from experience.
Abnormal behavior	An action, thought, or feeling that is harmful to the person or to others is called abnormal behavior.
Child development	Scientific study of the processes of change from conception through adolescence is called child development.
American Psychological Association	The American Psychological Association is a professional organization representing psychology in the US. The mission statement is to "advance psychology as a science and profession and as a means of promoting health, education , and human welfare".

65

Infancy	The developmental period that extends from birth to 18 or 24 months is called infancy.
Learning	Learning is a relatively permanent change in behavior that results from experience. Thus, to attribute a behavioral change to learning, the change must be relatively permanent and must result from experience.
Neonatal period	The first 4 weeks of life, a time of transition from intrauterine dependency to independent existence is called the neonatal period.
Reflex	A simple, involuntary response to a stimulus is referred to as reflex. Reflex actions originate at the spinal cord rather than the brain.
Skeletal muscle	Skeletal muscle is a type of striated muscle, attached to the skeleton. They are used to facilitate movement, by applying force to bones and joints; via contraction. They generally contract voluntarily (via nerve stimulation), although they can contract involuntarily.
Brain	The brain controls and coordinates most movement, behavior and homeostatic body functions such as heartbeat, blood pressure, fluid balance and body temperature. Functions of the brain are responsible for cognition, emotion, memory, motor learning and other sorts of learning. The brain is primarily made up of two types of cells: glia and neurons.
Tactile	Pertaining to the sense of touch is referred to as tactile.
Arnold Gesell	Arnold Gesell was a pioneer in the field of child development and developmental measurement. He constructed the Gesell dome, a one-way mirror shaped as a dome, under which children could be observed without being disturbed.
Stages	Stages represent relatively discrete periods of time in which functioning is qualitatively different from functioning at other periods.
Innate	Innate behavior is not learned or influenced by the environment, rather, it is present or predisposed at birth.
Variable	A variable refers to a measurable factor, characteristic, or attribute of an individual or a system.
Acquisition	Acquisition is the process of adapting to the environment, learning or becoming conditioned. In classical conditoning terms, it is the initial learning of the stimulus response link, which involves a neutral stimulus being associated with a unconditioned stimulus and becoming a conditioned stimulus.
Maturation	The orderly unfolding of traits, as regulated by the genetic code is called maturation.
Newell	Newell contributed to the Information Processing Language (1956) and two of the earliest AI programs, the Logic Theory Machine (1956) and the General Problem Solver (1957) (with Herbert Simon).
Enrichment	Deliberately making an environment more novel, complex, and perceptually or intellectually stimulating is referred to as enrichment.
Cephalocaudal	The sequence in which the greatest growth occurs at the top, the head, with physical growth in size, weight, and feature differentiation gradually working from top to bottom is referred to as a cephalocaudal pattern.
Toddler	A toddler is a child between the ages of one and three years old. During this period, the child learns a great deal about social roles and develops motor skills; to toddle is to walk unsteadily.
Central nervous system	The vertebrate central nervous system consists of the brain and spinal cord.
Sensorimotor	The first of Piaget's stages is the Sensorimotor stage. This stage typically ranges from

birth to 2 years. In this stage, children experience the world through their senses. During this stage, object permanence and stranger anxiety develop.

Perception	Perception is the process of acquiring, interpreting, selecting, and organizing sensory information.
Early Intervention	Early intervention is a process used to recognize warning signs for mental health problems and to take early action against factors that put individuals at risk.
Paradigm	Paradigm refers to the set of practices that defines a scientific discipline during a particular period of time. It provides a framework from which to conduct research, it ensures that a certain range of phenomena, those on which the paradigm focuses, are explored thoroughly. Itmay also blind scientists to other, perhaps more fruitful, ways of dealing with their subject matter.
Down syndrome	Down syndrome encompasses a number of genetic disorders, of which trisomy 21 (a nondisjunction, the so-called extrachromosone) is the most representative, causing highly variable degrees of learning difficulties as well as physical disabilities. Incidence of Down syndrome is estimated at 1 per 660 births, making it the most common chromosomal abnormality.
Critical period	A period of time when an innate response can be elicited by a particular stimulus is referred to as the critical period.
Seizure	A seizure is a temporary alteration in brain function expressed as a changed mental state, tonic or clonic movements and various other symptoms. They are due to temporary abnormal electrical activity of a group of brain cells.
Developmental level	An individual's current state of physical, emotional, and intellectual development is called the developmental level.
Preterm infant	An infant born before completing the thirty-seventh week of gestation is a preterm infant.

Learning	Learning is a relatively permanent change in behavior that results from experience. Thus, to attribute a behavioral change to learning, the change must be relatively permanent and must result from experience.
Perception	Perception is the process of acquiring, interpreting, selecting, and organizing sensory information.
Sensation	Sensation is the first stage in the chain of biochemical and neurologic events that begins with the impinging of a stimulus upon the receptor cells of a sensory organ, which then leads to perception, the mental state that is reflected in statements like "I see a uniformly blue wall."
Senses	The senses are systems that consist of a sensory cell type that respond to a specific kind of physical energy, and that correspond to a defined region within the brain where the signals are received and interpreted.
Tactile	Pertaining to the sense of touch is referred to as tactile.
Stimulus	A change in an environmental condition that elicits a response is a stimulus.
Reflex	A simple, involuntary response to a stimulus is referred to as reflex. Reflex actions originate at the spinal cord rather than the brain.
Pupil	In the eye, the pupil is the opening in the middle of the iris. It appears black because most of the light entering it is absorbed by the tissues inside the eye. The size of the pupil is controlled by involuntary contraction and dilation of the iris, in order to regulate the intensity of light entering the eye. This is known as the pupillary reflex.
Visual perception	Visual perception is one of the senses, consisting of the ability to detect light and interpret it. Vision has a specific sensory system.
Maturation	The orderly unfolding of traits, as regulated by the genetic code is called maturation.
Naturalistic observation	Naturalistic observation is a method of observation that involves observing subjects in their natural habitats. Researchers take great care in avoiding making interferences with the behavior they are observing by using unobtrusive methods.
Questionnaire	A self-report method of data collection or clinical assessment method in which the individual being studied checks off items on a printed list, answers multiple-choice questions, or writes out answers to essay questions aimed at producing a selfdescription is called questionnaire.
Attention	Attention is the cognitive process of selectively concentrating on one thing while ignoring other things. Psychologists have labeled three types of attention: sustained attention, selective attention, and divided attention.
Habituation	In habituation there is a progressive reduction in the response probability with continued repetition of a stimulus.
Dishabituation	A renewed interest in a stimulus is referred to as dishabituation.
Paradigm	Paradigm refers to the set of practices that defines a scientific discipline during a particular period of time. It provides a framework from which to conduct research, it ensures that a certain range of phenomena, those on which the paradigm focuses, are explored thoroughly. Itmay also blind scientists to other, perhaps more fruitful, ways of dealing with their subject matter.
Brain	The brain controls and coordinates most movement, behavior and homeostatic body functions such as heartbeat, blood pressure, fluid balance and body temperature. Functions of the brain are responsible for cognition, emotion, memory, motor learning and other sorts of learning. The brain is primarily made up of two types of cells: glia and neurons.

71

Electrode	Any device used to electrically stimulate nerve tissue or to record its activity is an electrode.
Central nervous system	The vertebrate central nervous system consists of the brain and spinal cord.
Chronological age	Chronological age refers to the number of years that have elapsed since a person's birth.
Fovea	The fovea, a part of the eye, is a spot located in the center of the macula. The fovea is responsible for sharp central vision, which is necessary in humans for reading, watching television or movies, driving, and any activity where visual detail is of primary importance.
Peripheral vision	Peripheral vision is that part of vision that occurs outside the very center of gaze. Peripheral vision is weak in humans, especially at distinguishing color and shape. This is because the density of receptor cells on the retina is greatest at the center and lowest at the edges
Visual acuity	Visual acuity is the eye's ability to detect fine details and is the quantitative measure of the eye's ability to see an in-focus image at a certain distance.
Accommodation	Piaget's developmental process of accommodation is the modification of currently held schemes or new schemes so that new information inconsistent with the existing schemes can be integrated and understood.
Fixation	Fixation in abnormal psychology is the state where an individual becomes obsessed with an attachment to another human, animal or inanimate object. Fixation in vision refers to maintaining the gaze in a constant direction. .
Discrimination	In Learning theory, discrimination refers the ability to distinguish between a conditioned stimulus and other stimuli. It can be brought about by extensive training or differential reinforcement. In social terms, it is the denial of privileges to a person or a group on the basis of prejudice.
Brightness	The dimension of visual sensation that is dependent on the intensity of light reflected from a surface and that corresponds to the amplitude of the light wave is called brightness.
Cornea	The cornea is the transparent front part of the eye that covers the iris, pupil, and anterior chamber and provides most of an eye's optical power. Together with the lens, the cornea refracts light and consequently helps the eye to focus.
Infancy	The developmental period that extends from birth to 18 or 24 months is called infancy.
Binocular vision	Binocular vision is vision in which both eyes are used synchronously to produce a single image. It confers two advantages over monocular vision: binocular summation in which the ability to detect faint objects is enhanced, and stereopsis in which parallax provided by the two eye's different positions on the head give precise depth perception.
Bifoveal fixation	The ability of the foveas of the two eyes to focus on the same object simultaneously, critical to binocular depth perception, is called bifoveal fixation.
Stereopsis	Stereopsis is the process in visual perception leading to perception of the depth or distance of objects. Depth from stereopsis arises from the slightly different positions each eye occupies on the head, a form of parallax.
Retina	The retina is a thin layer of cells at the back of the eyeball. It is the part of the eye which converts light into nervous signals. The retina contains photoreceptor cells which receive the light; the resulting neural signals then undergo complex processing by other neurons of the retina, and are transformed into action potentials in retinal ganglion cells whose axons form the optic nerve.

Retinal disparity	A binocular cue for depth based on the difference in the image cast by an object on the retinas of the eyes as the object moves closer or farther away, is called retinal disparity.
Monocular	Depth perception combines several types of depth clues grouped into two categories: monocular clues, available from the input of just one eye, and binocular clues. Monocular clues include motion parallax, color vision, perspective, relative size, distance fog, depth from focus, and occlusion
Postnatal	Postnatal is the period beginning immediately after the birth of a child and extending for about six weeks. The period is also known as postpartum and, less commonly, puerperium.
Research design	A research design tests a hypothesis. The basic typess are: descriptive, correlational, and experimental.
Depth cues	Perceptual features that impart information about distance and three-dimensional space are called depth cues.
Sensorimotor	The first of Piaget's stages is the Sensorimotor stage. This stage typically ranges from birth to 2 years. In this stage, children experience the world through their senses. During this stage, object permanence and stranger anxiety develop.
Visual cliff	An apparatus used to test depth perception in infants and young animals is the visual cliff. Infants, 6-14 months, were placed on the edge of the visual cliff, a small cliff with a drop-off covered by glass, to see if they would crawl over the edge. Most infants refused to crawl out on the glass signifying that they could perceive depth and that depth perception is not learned.
Feedback	Feedback refers to information returned to a person about the effects a response has had.
Necessary condition	A circumstance required for a particular phenomenon to occur is a necessary condition if and only if the condition does not occur in the absense of the circumstance.
Hue	A hue refers to the gradation of color within the optical spectrum, or visible spectrum, of light. Hue may also refer to a particular color within this spectrum, as defined by its dominant wavelength, or the central tendency of its combined wavelengths.
Rhodopsin	The photochemical in rods that undergoes structural changes in response to light and thereby initiates the transduction process for rod vision is rhodopsin. It most strongly absorbs green-blue light and therefore appears reddish-purple, which is why it is also called "visual purple".
Cones	Cones are photoreceptors that transmit sensations of color, function in bright light, and used in visual acuity. Infants prior to months of age can only distinguish green and red indicating the cones are not fully developed; they can see all of the colors by 2 months of
Rods	Rods are cylindrical shaped photoreceptors that are sensitive to the intensity of light. Rods require less light to function than cone cells, and therefore are the primary source of visual information at night.
Amniotic fluid	Amniotic fluid refers to fluid within the amniotic sac that suspends and protects the fetus.
Fetus	A fetus develops from the end of the 8th week of pregnancy (when the major structures have formed), until birth.
Loudness	Loudness is the quality of a sound that is the primary psychological correlate of physical intensity. Loudness is often approximated by a power function with an exponent of 0.6 when plotted vs. sound pressure or 0.3 when plotted vs. sound intensity.
Pitch	Pitch is the psychological interpretation of a sound or musical tone corresponding to its physical frequency

Affect	A subjective feeling or emotional tone often accompanied by bodily expressions noticeable to others is called affect.
Acquisition	Acquisition is the process of adapting to the environment, learning or becoming conditioned. In classical conditoning terms, it is the initial learning of the stimulus response link, which involves a neutral stimulus being associated with a unconditioned stimulus and becoming a conditioned stimulus.
Cognitive development	The process by which a child's understanding of the world changes as a function of age and experience is called cognitive development.
Threshold	In general, a threshold is a fixed location or value where an abrupt change is observed. In the sensory modalities, it is the minimum amount of stimulus energy necessary to elicit a sensory response.
Child development	Scientific study of the processes of change from conception through adolescence is called child development.
Nerve impulse	A nerve impulse is a change in the electric potential of a neuron; a wave of depolarization spreads along the neuron and causes the release of a neurotransmitter.
Neural network	A clusters of neurons that is interconnected to process information is referred to as a neural network.
Plasticity	The capacity for modification and change is referred to as plasticity.
Variability	Statistically, variability refers to how much the scores in a distribution spread out, away from the mean.
Early childhood	Early childhood refers to the developmental period extending from the end of infancy to about 5 or 6 years of age; sometimes called the preschool years.

Go to **Cram101.com** for the Practice Tests for this Chapter.

Adolescent growth spurt	The rapid increase in weight and height that occurs around the onset of puberty is referred to as the adolescent growth spurt.
Infancy	The developmental period that extends from birth to 18 or 24 months is called infancy.
Statistics	Statistics is a type of data analysis which practice includes the planning, summarizing, and interpreting of observations of a system possibly followed by predicting or forecasting of future events based on a mathematical model of the system being observed.
Statistic	A statistic is an observable random variable of a sample.
Puberty	Puberty refers to the process of physical changes by which a child's body becomes an adult body capable of reproduction.
Gender difference	A gender difference is a disparity between genders involving quality or quantity. Though some gender differences are controversial, they are not to be confused with sexist stereotypes.
Malnutrition	Malnutrition is a general term for the medical condition in a person or animal caused by an unbalanced diet—either too little or too much food, or a diet missing one or more important nutrients.
Cerebral cortex	The cerebral cortex is the outermost layer of the cerebrum and has a grey color. It is made up of four lobes and it is involved in many complex brain functions including memory, perceptual awareness, "thinking", language and consciousness. The cerebral cortex receives sensory information from many different sensory organs eg: eyes, ears, etc. and processes the information.
Midbrain	Located between the hindbrain and forebrain, a region in which many nerve-fiber systems ascend and descend to connect the higher and lower portions of the brain is referred to as midbrain. It is archipallian in origin, meaning its general architecture is shared with the most ancient of vertebrates. Dopamine produced in the subtantia nigra plays a role in motivation and habituation of species from humans to the most elementary animals such as insects.
Brain	The brain controls and coordinates most movement, behavior and homeostatic body functions such as heartbeat, blood pressure, fluid balance and body temperature. Functions of the brain are responsible for cognition, emotion, memory, motor learning and other sorts of learning. The brain is primarily made up of two types of cells: glia and neurons.
Nerve impulse	A nerve impulse is a change in the electric potential of a neuron; a wave of depolarization spreads along the neuron and causes the release of a neurotransmitter.
Myelination	The process in which the nerve cells are covered and insulated with a layer of fat cells, which increases the speed at which information travels through the nervous system is referred to as myelination.
Neuron	The neuron is the primary cell of the nervous system. They are found in the brain, the spinal cord, in the nerves and ganglia of the peripheral nervous system. It is a specialized cell that conducts impulses through the nervous system and contains three major parts: cell body, dendrites, and an axon. It can have many dendrites but only one axon.
Myelin	Myelin is an electrically insulating fatty layer that surrounds the axons of many neurons, especially those in the peripheral nervous system. The main consequence of a myelin sheath is an increase in the speed at which impulses propagate along the myelinated fiber. The sheath continues to develop throughout childhood.
Nerve	A nerve is an enclosed, cable-like bundle of nerve fibers or axons, which includes the glia that ensheath the axons in myelin. Neurons are sometimes called nerve cells, though this term is technically imprecise since many neurons do not form nerves.

Go to Cram101.com for the Practice Tests for this Chapter.

Transference	Transference is a phenomenon in psychology characterized by unconscious redirection of feelings from one person to another.
Nervous system	The body's electrochemical communication circuitry, made up of billions of neurons is a nervous system.
Cerebellum	The cerebellum is located in the inferior posterior portion of the head (the hindbrain), directly dorsal to the brainstem and pons, inferior to the occipital lobe. The cerebellum is a region of the brain that plays an important role in the integration of sensory perception and fine motor output.
Retina	The retina is a thin layer of cells at the back of the eyeball. It is the part of the eye which converts light into nervous signals. The retina contains photoreceptor cells which receive the light; the resulting neural signals then undergo complex processing by other neurons of the retina, and are transformed into action potentials in retinal ganglion cells whose axons form the optic nerve.
Taste bud	The taste bud (or lingual papillae) is a small structure on the upper surface of the tongue that provides information about the taste of food being eaten. It is known that there are five taste sensations: Sweet, Bitter, Umami, Salty and Sour.
Middle ear	The middle ear consists of the eardrum, hammer, anvil, and stirrup.
Gross motor skills	Gross motor skills refer to motor skills that involve large muscle activities, such as walking.
Affective	Affective is the way people react emotionally, their ability to feel another living thing's pain or joy.
Cognitive skills	Cognitive skills such as reasoning, attention, and memory can be advanced and sustained through practice and training.
Perception	Perception is the process of acquiring, interpreting, selecting, and organizing sensory information.
Cognitive development	The process by which a child's understanding of the world changes as a function of age and experience is called cognitive development.
Cognitive structure	According to Piaget, the number of schemata available to an organism at any given time constitutes that organism's cognitive structure. How the organism interacts with its environment depends on the current cognitive structure available. As the cognitive structure develops, new assimilations can occur.
Variable	A variable refers to a measurable factor, characteristic, or attribute of an individual or a system.
Autonomy	Autonomy is the condition of something that does not depend on anything else.
Guilt	Guilt describes many concepts related to a negative emotion or condition caused by actions which are believed to be, morally wrong. According to Freud, the avoidance of guilt is the basis for moral behavior.
Self-concept	Self-concept refers to domain-specific evaluations of the self where a domain may be academics, athletics, etc.
Homeostasis	Homeostasis is the property of an open system, especially living organisms, to regulate its internal environment so as to maintain a stable condition, by means of multiple dynamic equilibrium adjustments controlled by interrelated regulation mechanisms.
Farsightedness	Hyperopia, also known as farsightedness, is a defect of vision caused by an imperfection in the eye (often when the eyeball is too short), causing inability to focus on near objects,

Go to **Cram101.com** for the Practice Tests for this Chapter.

and in extreme cases causing a sufferer to be unable to focus on objects at any distance.

Learning	Learning is a relatively permanent change in behavior that results from experience. Thus, to attribute a behavioral change to learning, the change must be relatively permanent and must result from experience.
Positive reinforcement	In positive reinforcement, a stimulus is added and the rate of responding increases.
Creativity	Creativity is the ability to think about something in novel and unusual ways and come up with unique solutions to problems. It involves divergent thinking, having many solutions or views to a problem.
Individual differences	Individual differences psychology studies the ways in which individual people differ in their behavior. This is distinguished from other aspects of psychology in that although psychology is ostensibly a study of individuals, modern psychologists invariably study groups.
Developmental level	An individual's current state of physical, emotional, and intellectual development is called the developmental level.
Sensorimotor	The first of Piaget's stages is the Sensorimotor stage. This stage typically ranges from birth to 2 years. In this stage, children experience the world through their senses. During this stage, object permanence and stranger anxiety develop.
Visual acuity	Visual acuity is the eye's ability to detect fine details and is the quantitative measure of the eye's ability to see an in-focus image at a certain distance.
Attention	Attention is the cognitive process of selectively concentrating on one thing while ignoring other things. Psychologists have labeled three types of attention: sustained attention, selective attention, and divided attention.
Cephalocaudal	The sequence in which the greatest growth occurs at the top, the head, with physical growth in size, weight, and feature differentiation gradually working from top to bottom is referred to as a cephalocaudal pattern.
Proximodistal	Development originating from the center of the body towards the extremities is referred to as proximodistal development. The human embroyo normally develops in this fashion and averages 5-10 pounds in brith-weight and between 18 to 22 inches in length.
Reaction time	The amount of time required to respond to a stimulus is referred to as reaction time.
Reinforcement	In operant conditioning, reinforcement is any change in an environment that (a) occurs after the behavior, (b) seems to make that behavior re-occur more often in the future and (c) that reoccurence of behavior must be the result of the change.
Punishment	Punishment is the addtion of a stimulus that reduces the frequency of a response, or the removal of a stimulus that results in a reduction of the response.
Critical thinking	Critical thinking is a mental process of analyzing or evaluating information, particularly statements or propositions that are offered as true.
Heredity	Heredity is the transfer of characteristics from parent to offspring through their genes.
Affect	A subjective feeling or emotional tone often accompanied by bodily expressions noticeable to others is called affect.
Prenatal	Prenatal period refers to the time from conception to birth.
Adolescence	The period of life bounded by puberty and the assumption of adult responsibilities is adolescence.
Lesion	A lesion is a non-specific term referring to abnormal tissue in the body. It can be caused by

Go to **Cram101.com** for the Practice Tests for this Chapter.

any disease process including trauma (physical, chemical, electrical), infection, neoplasm, metabolic and autoimmune.

Chronic	Chronic refers to a relatively long duration, usually more than a few months.
Kwashiorkor	Kwashiorkor is a childhood disorder caused by lack of nutrients, including protein in the diet. Symptoms of kwashiorkor include a swollen abdomen, reddish discoloration of the hair and depigmented skin.
Norms	In testing, standards of test performance that permit the comparison of one person's score on the test to the scores of others who have taken the same test are referred to as norms.
Ethnic group	An ethnic group is a culture or subculture whose members are readily distinguishable by outsiders based on traits originating from a common racial, national, linguistic, or religious source. Members of an ethnic group are often presumed to be culturally or biologically similar, although this is not in fact necessarily the case.
Obesity	The state of being more than 20 percent above the average weight for a person of one's height is called obesity.
Hypothesis	A specific statement about behavior or mental processes that is testable through research is a hypothesis.
Habit	A habit is a response that has become completely separated from its eliciting stimulus. Early learning theorists used the term to describe S-R associations, however not all S-R associations become a habit, rather many are extinguished after reinforcement is withdrawn.
Reinforcer	In operant conditioning, a reinforcer is any stimulus that increases the probability that a preceding behavior will occur again. In Classical Conditioning, the unconditioned stimulus (US) is the reinforcer.
Addiction	Addiction is an uncontrollable compulsion to repeat a behavior regardless of its consequences. Many drugs or behaviors can precipitate a pattern of conditions recognized as addiction, which include a craving for more of the drug or behavior, increased physiological tolerance to exposure, and withdrawal symptoms in the absence of the stimulus.
Disuse	Disuse refers to theory that memory traces weaken when memories are not periodically used or retrieved.
Maturation	The orderly unfolding of traits, as regulated by the genetic code is called maturation.
Ectomorphic	The ectomorphic body type is centered around the brain and nerves. These people are slim. The ectomorfic person has a cerebrotonic temperament, and is artistic, sensitive, apprehensive and highly self-aware. A more negative way to put it is that he or she is introverted and socially restrained.
Endomorphic	The endomorphic body type is centered around the digestive system and is easily overweight. The endomorphic person also has a visceral temperament, which means that they are tolerant, love comfort and luxury, and are extroverted - in short he or she loves food and people.
Mesomorphic	The mesomorphic body type is centered around muscle and the circulatory system and has well developed muscles. The mesomorphic person has a somatotonic temperament, and is courageous, energetic, active, dynamic, assertive, aggressive, competitive, and often a risk taker.
Acute	Acute means sudden, sharp, and abrupt. Usually short in duration.
Emotion	An emotion is a mental states that arise spontaneously, rather than through conscious effort. They are often accompanied by physiological changes.
Measles	Measles, also known as rubeola, is a common disease caused by a virus of the genus Morbillivirus. Complications with measles are relatively common, ranging from relatively

Go to **Cram101.com** for the Practice Tests for this Chapter.
And, **NEVER** highlight a book again!

common and less serious diarrhea, to pneumonia and encephalitis. Complications are usually more severe amongst infants and adults who catch the virus.

Mumps

Mumps is a viral disease. It usually causes painful enlargement of the salivary or parotid glands.

Secular trend

A secular trend is change that occurs with respect to time.

Reflection

Reflection is the process of rephrasing or repeating thoughts and feelings expressed, making the person more aware of what they are saying or thinking.

Socioeconomic

Socioeconomic pertains to the study of the social and economic impacts of any product or service offering, market intervention or other activity on an economy as a whole and on the companies, organization and individuals who are its main economic actors.

Population

Population refers to all members of a well-defined group of organisms, events, or things.

Menarche

Menarche is the first menstrual period as a girl's body progresses through the changes of puberty. Menarche usually occurs about two years after the first changes of breast development.

Infancy	The developmental period that extends from birth to 18 or 24 months is called infancy.
Perception	Perception is the process of acquiring, interpreting, selecting, and organizing sensory information.
Acquisition	Acquisition is the process of adapting to the environment, learning or becoming conditioned. In classical conditoning terms, it is the initial learning of the stimulus response link, which involves a neutral stimulus being associated with a unconditioned stimulus and becoming a conditioned stimulus.
Early childhood	Early childhood refers to the developmental period extending from the end of infancy to about 5 or 6 years of age; sometimes called the preschool years.
Normative	The term normative is used to describe the effects of those structures of culture which regulate the function of social activity.
Stage theory	Stage theory characterizes development by hypothesizing the existence of distinct, and often critical, periods of life. Each period follows one another in an orderly sequence.
Stages	Stages represent relatively discrete periods of time in which functioning is qualitatively different from functioning at other periods.
Maturation	The orderly unfolding of traits, as regulated by the genetic code is called maturation.
Learning	Learning is a relatively permanent change in behavior that results from experience. Thus, to attribute a behavioral change to learning, the change must be relatively permanent and must result from experience.
Affect	A subjective feeling or emotional tone often accompanied by bodily expressions noticeable to others is called affect.
Control group	A group that does not receive the treatment effect in an experiment is referred to as the control group or sometimes as the comparison group.
Quantitative	A quantitative property is one that exists in a range of magnitudes, and can therefore be measured. Measurements of any particular quantitative property are expressed as as a specific quantity, referred to as a unit, multiplied by a number.
Individuality	According to Cooper, individuality consists of two dimensions: self-assertion and separateness.
Sensorimotor	The first of Piaget's stages is the Sensorimotor stage. This stage typically ranges from birth to 2 years. In this stage, children experience the world through their senses. During this stage, object permanence and stranger anxiety develop.
Semicircular canals	The semicircular canals are three half-circular, interconnected tubes located inside each ear that are the equivalent of three gyroscopes located in three planes perpendicular (at right angles) to each other.
Elaboration	The extensiveness of processing at any given level of memory is called elaboration. The use of elaboration changes developmentally. Adolescents are more likely to use elaboration spontaneously than children.
Reaction time	The amount of time required to respond to a stimulus is referred to as reaction time.
Projection	Attributing one's own undesirable thoughts, impulses, traits, or behaviors to others is referred to as projection.
Attention	Attention is the cognitive process of selectively concentrating on one thing while ignoring other things. Psychologists have labeled three types of attention: sustained attention, selective attention, and divided attention.

Go to **Cram101.com** for the Practice Tests for this Chapter.

Ion	An ion is an atom or group of atoms with a net electric charge. The energy required to detach an electron in its lowest energy state from an atom or molecule of a gas with less net electric charge is called the ionization potential, or ionization energy.
Tact	The word tact, another of Skinner's intentionally "nonsense" words, comes from the notion of the child's making "conTACT" with the nonverbal environment. The tact is verbal behavior that is under the control of the nonverbal environment and includes nouns, actions, adjectives, pronouns, relations, and others.
Pitch	Pitch is the psychological interpretation of a sound or musical tone corresponding to its physical frequency
Figure-ground	The Gestalt principle of Figure-ground states that there is an innate tendency to perceive one aspect of an event as the figure or foreground and the other as the ground or the background.
Developmental level	An individual's current state of physical, emotional, and intellectual development is called the developmental level.
Dynamic Systems Theory	Dynamic Systems Theory believes that in order to develop motor skills, infants must perceive something in the environment that motivates them to act, and they must use their perceptions to fine-tune their movements. Motor skills represent solutions to the infant's goals. The behavior is the result of many converging factors.

Go to **Cram101.com** for the Practice Tests for this Chapter.

Statistics	Statistics is a type of data analysis which practice includes the planning, summarizing, and interpreting of observations of a system possibly followed by predicting or forecasting of future events based on a mathematical model of the system being observed.
Statistic	A statistic is an observable random variable of a sample.
Survey	A method of scientific investigation in which a large sample of people answer questions about their attitudes or behavior is referred to as a survey.
Wisdom	Wisdom is the ability to make correct judgments and decisions. It is an intangible quality gained through experience. Whether or not something is wise is determined in a pragmatic sense by its popularity, how long it has been around, and its ability to predict against future events.
Mental retardation	Mental retardation refers to having significantly below-average intellectual functioning and limitations in at least two areas of adaptive functioning. Many categorize retardation as mild, moderate, severe, or profound.
Cholesterol	Cholesterol is a steroid, a lipid, and an alcohol, found in the cell membranes of all body tissues, and transported in the blood plasma of all animals. Cholesterol is an important component of the membranes of cells, providing stability; it makes the membrane's fluidity stable over a bigger temperature interval.
Obesity	The state of being more than 20 percent above the average weight for a person of one's height is called obesity.
Norms	In testing, standards of test performance that permit the comparison of one person's score on the test to the scores of others who have taken the same test are referred to as norms.
Lungs	The lungs are the essential organs of respiration. Its principal function is to transport oxygen from the atmosphere into the bloodstream, and excrete carbon dioxide from the bloodstream into the atmosphere.
Puberty	Puberty refers to the process of physical changes by which a child's body becomes an adult body capable of reproduction.
Reliability	Reliability means the extent to which a test produces a consistent , reproducible score .
Longitudinal studies	Investigation that collects information on the same individuals repeatedly over time, perhaps over many years, in an effort to determine how phenomena change is referred to as longitudinal studies. These studies to to be time consuming and expensive.
Threshold	In general, a threshold is a fixed location or value where an abrupt change is observed. In the sensory modalities, it is the minimum amount of stimulus energy necessary to elicit a sensory response.
Validity	The extent to which a test measures what it is intended to measure is called validity.
Emotion	An emotion is a mental states that arise spontaneously, rather than through conscious effort. They are often accompanied by physiological changes.
Direct observation	Direct observation refers to assessing behavior through direct surveillance.
Regression	Return to a form of behavior characteristic of an earlier stage of development is called regression.
Predictive validity	Predictive validity refers to the relation between test scores and the student 's future performance .
Adolescence	The period of life bounded by puberty and the assumption of adult responsibilities is adolescence.

Variability	Statistically, variability refers to how much the scores in a distribution spread out, away from the mean.
Chronological age	Chronological age refers to the number of years that have elapsed since a person's birth.
Habit	A habit is a response that has become completely separated from its eliciting stimulus. Early learning theorists used the term to describe S-R associations, however not all S-R associations become a habit, rather many are extinguished after reinforcement is withdrawn.
Knowledge base	The general background information a person possesses, which influences most cognitive task performance is called the knowledge base.
Conditioning	Conditioning describes the process by which behaviors can be learned or modified through interaction with the environment.
Attention	Attention is the cognitive process of selectively concentrating on one thing while ignoring other things. Psychologists have labeled three types of attention: sustained attention, selective attention, and divided attention.
Hypothesis	A specific statement about behavior or mental processes that is testable through research is a hypothesis.
Androgen	Androgen is the generic term for any natural or synthetic compound, usually a steroid hormone, that stimulates or controls the development and maintenance of masculine characteristics in vertebrates by binding to androgen receptors.
Hormone	A hormone is a chemical messenger from one cell (or group of cells) to another. The best known are those produced by endocrine glands, but they are produced by nearly every organ system. The function of hormones is to serve as a signal to the target cells; the action of the hormone is determined by the pattern of secretion and the signal transduction of the receiving tissue.
Growth hormone	Growth hormone is a polypeptide hormone synthesised and secreted by the anterior pituitary gland which stimulates growth and cell reproduction in humans and other vertebrate animals.
Protein	A protein is a complex, high-molecular-weight organic compound that consists of amino acids joined by peptide bonds. It is essential to the structure and function of all living cells and viruses. Many are enzymes or subunits of enzymes.
Identical twins	Identical twins occur when a single egg is fertilized to form one zygote (monozygotic) but the zygote then divides into two separate embryos. The two embryos develop into foetuses sharing the same womb. Monozygotic twins are genetically identical unless there has been a mutation in development, and they are almost always the same gender.
Population	Population refers to all members of a well-defined group of organisms, events, or things.
Testosterone	Testosterone is a steroid hormone from the androgen group. It is the principal male sex hormone and the "original" anabolic steroid.
Central nervous system	The vertebrate central nervous system consists of the brain and spinal cord.
Maturation	The orderly unfolding of traits, as regulated by the genetic code is called maturation.
Adaptation	Adaptation is a lowering of sensitivity to a stimulus following prolonged exposure to that stimulus. Behavioral adaptations are special ways a particular organism behaves to survive in its natural habitat.
Correlation	A statistical technique for determining the degree of association between two or more variables is referred to as correlation.

Go to **Cram101.com** for the Practice Tests for this Chapter.

Chronic	Chronic refers to a relatively long duration, usually more than a few months.
Variable	A variable refers to a measurable factor, characteristic, or attribute of an individual or a system.
Reciprocity	Reciprocity, in interpersonal attraction, is the tendency to return feelings and attitudes that are expressed about us.
Early childhood	Early childhood refers to the developmental period extending from the end of infancy to about 5 or 6 years of age; sometimes called the preschool years.
Acquisition	Acquisition is the process of adapting to the environment, learning or becoming conditioned. In classical conditoning terms, it is the initial learning of the stimulus response link, which involves a neutral stimulus being associated with a unconditioned stimulus and becoming a conditioned stimulus.
Semicircular canals	The semicircular canals are three half-circular, interconnected tubes located inside each ear that are the equivalent of three gyroscopes located in three planes perpendicular (at right angles) to each other.
Otolith	The otolith organs (the utricle and the saccule) are structures in the inner ear that are sensitive to gravity and linear acceleration. Because of their orientation in the head, the utricle is sensitive to a change in horizontal movement, and the saccule gives information about vertical acceleration (such as when in an elevator).
Nerve impulse	A nerve impulse is a change in the electric potential of a neuron; a wave of depolarization spreads along the neuron and causes the release of a neurotransmitter.
Receptor	A sensory receptor is a structure that recognizes a stimulus in the internal or external environment of an organism. In response to stimuli the sensory receptor initiates sensory transduction by creating graded potentials or action potentials in the same cell or in an adjacent one.
Macula	The macula is an oval yellow spot near the center of the retina of the human eye. Near its center is the fovea, a small pit that contains the largest concentration of cone cells in the eye and is responsible for central vision.
Nerve	A nerve is an enclosed, cable-like bundle of nerve fibers or axons, which includes the glia that ensheath the axons in myelin. Neurons are sometimes called nerve cells, though this term is technically imprecise since many neurons do not form nerves.
Kinesthetic system	The kinesthetic system is the sense of the position of parts of the body, relative to other neighbouring parts of the body. It is a sense that provides feedback solely on the status of the body internally.
Tactile	Pertaining to the sense of touch is referred to as tactile.
Reaction time	The amount of time required to respond to a stimulus is referred to as reaction time.
Gender difference	A gender difference is a disparity between genders involving quality or quantity. Though some gender differences are controversial, they are not to be confused with sexist stereotypes.
Randomization	Method for placing individuals into research groups that assures each one of an equal chance of being assigned to any group, to eliminate any systematic differences across groups is referred to as randomization.
Meta-analysis	In statistics, a meta-analysis combines the results of several studies that address a set of related research hypotheses.

Go to **Cram101.com** for the Practice Tests for this Chapter.

Cognition	The intellectual processes through which information is obtained, transformed, stored, retrieved, and otherwise used is cognition.
Perception	Perception is the process of acquiring, interpreting, selecting, and organizing sensory information.
Brain	The brain controls and coordinates most movement, behavior and homeostatic body functions such as heartbeat, blood pressure, fluid balance and body temperature. Functions of the brain are responsible for cognition, emotion, memory, motor learning and other sorts of learning. The brain is primarily made up of two types of cells: glia and neurons.
Occipital lobe	The occipital lobe is the smallest of four true lobes in the human brain. Located in the rearmost portion of the skull, the occipital lobe is part of the forebrain structure. It is the visual processing center.
Parietal lobe	The parietal lobe is positioned above (superior to) the occipital lobe and behind (posterior to) the frontal lobe. It plays important roles in integrating sensory information from various senses, and in the manipulation of objects.
Frontal lobe	The frontal lobe comprises four major folds of cortical tissue: the precentral gyrus, superior gyrus and the middle gyrus of the frontal gyri, the inferior frontal gyrus. It has been found to play a part in impulse control, judgement, language, memory, motor function, problem solving, sexual behavior, socialization and spontaneity.
Sensation	Sensation is the first stage in the chain of biochemical and neurologic events that begins with the impinging of a stimulus upon the receptor cells of a sensory organ, which then leads to perception, the mental state that is reflected in statements like "I see a uniformly blue wall."
Cerebellum	The cerebellum is located in the inferior posterior portion of the head (the hindbrain), directly dorsal to the brainstem and pons, inferior to the occipital lobe. The cerebellum is a region of the brain that plays an important role in the integration of sensory perception and fine motor output.
Figure-ground	The Gestalt principle of Figure-ground states that there is an innate tendency to perceive one aspect of an event as the figure or foreground and the other as the ground or the background.
Hypothesis	A specific statement about behavior or mental processes that is testable through research is a hypothesis.
Deprivation experiment	An experiment in which animals are raised in ways that deprive them of some of their usual experiences in order to determine what experiences are essential for a particular species-typical behavior to develop is a called a deprivation experiment.
Attention	Attention is the cognitive process of selectively concentrating on one thing while ignoring other things. Psychologists have labeled three types of attention: sustained attention, selective attention, and divided attention.
Hebb	Hebb demonstrated that the rearing of rats in an enriched environment could alter neural development and that sensory - neural connections were shaped by experience. He is famous for developing the concept of neural nets. He also believed that learning early in life is of the incremental variety, whereas later it is cognitive, insightful, and more all-or-none.
Sufficient condition	To say that A is a sufficient condition for B is to say precisely the converse: that A cannot occur without B, or whenever A occurs, B occurs. That there is a fire is sufficient for there being smoke.
Necessary condition	A circumstance required for a particular phenomenon to occur is a necessary condition if and only if the condition does not occur in the absense of the circumstance.

Go to **Cram101.com** for the Practice Tests for this Chapter.

Developmental level	An individual's current state of physical, emotional, and intellectual development is called the developmental level.
Affect	A subjective feeling or emotional tone often accompanied by bodily expressions noticeable to others is called affect.
Learning	Learning is a relatively permanent change in behavior that results from experience. Thus, to attribute a behavioral change to learning, the change must be relatively permanent and must result from experience.
Visual acuity	Visual acuity is the eye's ability to detect fine details and is the quantitative measure of the eye's ability to see an in-focus image at a certain distance.
Ion	An ion is an atom or group of atoms with a net electric charge. The energy required to detach an electron in its lowest energy state from an atom or molecule of a gas with less net electric charge is called the ionization potential, or ionization energy.
Socialization	Social rules and social relations are created, communicated, and changed in verbal and nonverbal ways creating social complexity useful in identifying outsiders and intelligent breeding partners. The process of learning these skills is called socialization.
Maturation	The orderly unfolding of traits, as regulated by the genetic code is called maturation.
Visual perception	Visual perception is one of the senses, consisting of the ability to detect light and interpret it. Vision has a specific sensory system.
Depth cues	Perceptual features that impart information about distance and three-dimensional space are called depth cues.
Monocular	Depth perception combines several types of depth clues grouped into two categories: monocular clues, available from the input of just one eye, and binocular clues. Monocular clues include motion parallax, color vision, perspective, relative size, distance fog, depth from focus, and occlusion
Binocular depth cues	Binocular depth cues that depend on two eyes working together.
Retinal disparity	A binocular cue for depth based on the difference in the image cast by an object on the retinas of the eyes as the object moves closer or farther away, is called retinal disparity.
Binocular vision	Binocular vision is vision in which both eyes are used synchronously to produce a single image. It confers two advantages over monocular vision: binocular summation in which the ability to detect faint objects is enhanced, and stereopsis in which parallax provided by the two eye's different positions on the head give precise depth perception.
Stages	Stages represent relatively discrete periods of time in which functioning is qualitatively different from functioning at other periods.
Infancy	The developmental period that extends from birth to 18 or 24 months is called infancy.
Confounding variable	A confounding variable is a variable which is the common cause of two things that may falsely appear to be in a causal relationship. It is the cause of a spurious relationship.
Innate	Innate behavior is not learned or influenced by the environment, rather, it is present or predisposed at birth.
Perceptual learning	Perceptual learning refers to changes in perception that can be attributed to experience.
Plasticity	The capacity for modification and change is referred to as plasticity.
Society	The social sciences use the term society to mean a group of people that form a semi-closed

	(or semi-open) social system, in which most interactions are with other individuals belonging to the group.
Habit	A habit is a response that has become completely separated from its eliciting stimulus. Early learning theorists used the term to describe S-R associations, however not all S-R associations become a habit, rather many are extinguished after reinforcement is withdrawn.
Adaptation	Adaptation is a lowering of sensitivity to a stimulus following prolonged exposure to that stimulus. Behavioral adaptations are special ways a particular organism behaves to survive in its natural habitat.
Feedback	Feedback refers to information returned to a person about the effects a response has had.
Long-term memory	Long-term memory is memory that lasts from over 30 seconds to years.
Tactile	Pertaining to the sense of touch is referred to as tactile.
Acquisition	Acquisition is the process of adapting to the environment, learning or becoming conditioned. In classical conditoning terms, it is the initial learning of the stimulus response link, which involves a neutral stimulus being associated with a unconditioned stimulus and becoming a conditioned stimulus.
Body image	A person's body image is their perception of their physical appearance. It is more than what a person thinks they will see in a mirror, it is inextricably tied to their self-esteem and acceptance by peers.
Schema	Schema refers to a way of mentally representing the world, such as a belief or an expectation, that can influence perception of persons, objects, and situations.
Anorexia	Anorexia nervosa is an eating disorder characterized by voluntary starvation and exercise stress.
Bulimia	Bulimia refers to a disorder in which a person binges on incredibly large quantities of food, then purges by vomiting or by using laxatives. Bulimia is often less about food, and more to do with deep psychological issues and profound feelings of lack of control.
Self-esteem	Self-esteem refers to a person's subjective appraisal of himself or herself as intrinsically positive or negative to some degree.
Concrete operations	In Piaget's theory, the third major stage of cognitive development, in which children can decenter their perception, are less egocentric, and can think logically about concrete objects is called concrete operations.
Cognitive structure	According to Piaget, the number of schemata available to an organism at any given time constitutes that organism's cognitive structure. How the organism interacts with its environment depends on the current cognitive structure available. As the cognitive structure develops, new assimilations can occur.
Cognitive development	The process by which a child's understanding of the world changes as a function of age and experience is called cognitive development.
Piaget	Piaget argued that young children's answers were qualitatively different than older children rather than quantitative. There are two major aspects to his theory: the process of coming to know and the stages we move through as we gradually acquire this ability.
Projection	Attributing one's own undesirable thoughts, impulses, traits, or behaviors to others is referred to as projection.
Reinforcement	In operant conditioning, reinforcement is any change in an environment that (a) occurs after the behavior, (b) seems to make that behavior re-occur more often in the future and (c) that reoccurence of behavior must be the result of the change.

Acute	Acute means sudden, sharp, and abrupt. Usually short in duration.
Variability	Statistically, variability refers to how much the scores in a distribution spread out, away from the mean.
Elaboration	The extensiveness of processing at any given level of memory is called elaboration. The use of elaboration changes developmentally. Adolescents are more likely to use elaboration spontaneously than children.
Occupational therapists	Occupational therapists work with the disabled, the elderly, newborns, school-aged children, and with anyone who has a permanent or temporary impairment in their physical or mental functioning.
Affordance	An affordance is a property of an object, or a feature of the immediate environment, that indicates how that object or feature can be interfaced with. The empty space within an open doorway, for instance, affords movement across that threshold.
Validity	The extent to which a test measures what it is intended to measure is called validity.
Variable	A variable refers to a measurable factor, characteristic, or attribute of an individual or a system.
Scientific research	Research that is objective, systematic, and testable is called scientific research.
Developmentally disabled	developmentally disabled is a term for a pattern of persistently slow learning of basic motor and language skills during childhood, and a significantly below-normal global intellectual capacity as an adult.
Task analysis	The procedure of identifying the component elements of a behavior chain is called task analysis.
Empirical	Empirical means the use of working hypotheses which are capable of being disproved using observation or experiment.

Affective	Affective is the way people react emotionally, their ability to feel another living thing's pain or joy.
Self-concept	Self-concept refers to domain-specific evaluations of the self where a domain may be academics, athletics, etc.
William James	Functionalism as a psychology developed out of Pragmatism as a philosophy: To find the meaning of an idea, you have to look at its consequences. This led William James and his students towards an emphasis on cause and effect, prediction and control, and observation of environment and behavior, over the careful introspection of the Structuralists.
Self-esteem	Self-esteem refers to a person's subjective appraisal of himself or herself as intrinsically positive or negative to some degree.
Self-worth	In psychology, self-esteem or self-worth refers to a person's subjective appraisal of himself or herself as intrinsically positive or negative to some degree.
Attitude	An enduring mental representation of a person, place, or thing that evokes an emotional response and related behavior is called attitude.
Self-efficacy	Self-efficacy is the belief that one has the capabilities to execute the courses of actions required to manage prospective situations.
Bandura	Bandura is best known for his work on social learning theory or Social Cognitivism. His famous Bobo doll experiment illustrated that people learn from observing others.
Perception	Perception is the process of acquiring, interpreting, selecting, and organizing sensory information.
Achievement motivation	The psychological need in humans for success is called achievement motivation.
Society	The social sciences use the term society to mean a group of people that form a semi-closed (or semi-open) social system, in which most interactions are with other individuals belonging to the group.
Questionnaire	A self-report method of data collection or clinical assessment method in which the individual being studied checks off items on a printed list, answers multiple-choice questions, or writes out answers to essay questions aimed at producing a selfdescription is called questionnaire.
Infancy	The developmental period that extends from birth to 18 or 24 months is called infancy.
Attention	Attention is the cognitive process of selectively concentrating on one thing while ignoring other things. Psychologists have labeled three types of attention: sustained attention, selective attention, and divided attention.
Longitudinal study	Longitudinal study refers to a type of developmental study in which the same group of participants is followed and measured at different ages on some set of behaviors.
Adaptation	Adaptation is a lowering of sensitivity to a stimulus following prolonged exposure to that stimulus. Behavioral adaptations are special ways a particular organism behaves to survive in its natural habitat.
Erik Erikson	Erik Erikson conceived eight stages of development, each confronting the individual with its own psychosocial demands, that continued into old age. Personality development, according to Erikson, takes place through a series of crises that must be overcome and internalized by the individual in preparation for the next developmental stage. Such crisis are not catastrophes but vulnerabilities.
Toddler	A toddler is a child between the ages of one and three years old. During this period, the

	child learns a great deal about social roles and develops motor skills; to toddle is to walk unsteadily.
Autonomy	Autonomy is the condition of something that does not depend on anything else.
Early childhood	Early childhood refers to the developmental period extending from the end of infancy to about 5 or 6 years of age; sometimes called the preschool years.
Individuality	According to Cooper, individuality consists of two dimensions: self-assertion and separateness.
Learning	Learning is a relatively permanent change in behavior that results from experience. Thus, to attribute a behavioral change to learning, the change must be relatively permanent and must result from experience.
Affect	A subjective feeling or emotional tone often accompanied by bodily expressions noticeable to others is called affect.
Creativity	Creativity is the ability to think about something in novel and unusual ways and come up with unique solutions to problems. It involves divergent thinking, having many solutions or views to a problem.
Acquisition	Acquisition is the process of adapting to the environment, learning or becoming conditioned. In classical conditoning terms, it is the initial learning of the stimulus response link, which involves a neutral stimulus being associated with a unconditioned stimulus and becoming a conditioned stimulus.
Self-understanding	Self-understanding is a child's cognitive representation of the self, the substance and content of the child's self-conceptions.
Motivation	In psychology, motivation is the driving force (desire) behind all actions of an organism.
Variable	A variable refers to a measurable factor, characteristic, or attribute of an individual or a system.
Cross-sectional study	A type of developmental study in which researchers compare groups of participants of different ages on certain characteristics to determine age related differences is called a cross-sectional study.
Maladjustment	Maladjustment is the condition of being unable to adapt properly to your environment with resulting emotional instability.
Shaping	The concept of reinforcing successive, increasingly accurate approximations to a target behavior is called shaping. The target behavior is broken down into a hierarchy of elemental steps, each step more sophisticated then the last. By successively reinforcing each of the the elemental steps, a form of differential reinforcement, until that step is learned while extinguishing the step below, the target behavior is gradually achieved.
Correlation	A statistical technique for determining the degree of association between two or more variables is referred to as correlation.
Self-image	A person's self-image is the mental picture, generally of a kind that is quite resistant to change, that depicts not only details that are potentially available to objective investigation by others, but also items that have been learned by that person about himself or herself.
Anxiety	Anxiety is a complex combination of the feeling of fear, apprehension and worry often accompanied by physical sensations such as palpitations, chest pain and/or shortness of breath.
Stages	Stages represent relatively discrete periods of time in which functioning is qualitatively

different from functioning at other periods.

Problem solving	An attempt to find an appropriate way of attaining a goal when the goal is not readily available is called problem solving.
Individual differences	Individual differences psychology studies the ways in which individual people differ in their behavior. This is distinguished from other aspects of psychology in that although psychology is ostensibly a study of individuals, modern psychologists invariably study groups.
Reliability	Reliability means the extent to which a test produces a consistent , reproducible score .
Validity	The extent to which a test measures what it is intended to measure is called validity.
Child development	Scientific study of the processes of change from conception through adolescence is called child development.
Skeletal muscle	Skeletal muscle is a type of striated muscle, attached to the skeleton. They are used to facilitate movement, by applying force to bones and joints; via contraction. They generally contract voluntarily (via nerve stimulation), although they can contract involuntarily.
Testosterone	Testosterone is a steroid hormone from the androgen group. It is the principal male sex hormone and the "original" anabolic steroid.
Maturation	The orderly unfolding of traits, as regulated by the genetic code is called maturation.
Puberty	Puberty refers to the process of physical changes by which a child's body becomes an adult body capable of reproduction.
Hormone	A hormone is a chemical messenger from one cell (or group of cells) to another. The best known are those produced by endocrine glands, but they are produced by nearly every organ system. The function of hormones is to serve as a signal to the target cells; the action of the hormone is determined by the pattern of secretion and the signal transduction of the receiving tissue.
Estrogen	Estrogen is a group of steroid compounds that function as the primary female sex hormone. They are produced primarily by developing follicles in the ovaries, the corpus luteum and the placenta.
Androgen	Androgen is the generic term for any natural or synthetic compound, usually a steroid hormone, that stimulates or controls the development and maintenance of masculine characteristics in vertebrates by binding to androgen receptors.
Estradiol	Estradiol is a sex hormone. Labelled the "female" hormone but also present in males it represents the major estrogen in humans. Critical for sexual functioning estradiol also supports bone growth.
Early adulthood	The developmental period beginning in the late teens or early twenties and lasting into the thirties is called early adulthood; characterized by an increasing self-awareness.
Adolescence	The period of life bounded by puberty and the assumption of adult responsibilities is adolescence.

Go to **Cram101.com** for the Practice Tests for this Chapter.

Maturation	The orderly unfolding of traits, as regulated by the genetic code is called maturation.
Society	The social sciences use the term society to mean a group of people that form a semi-closed (or semi-open) social system, in which most interactions are with other individuals belonging to the group.
Puberty	Puberty refers to the process of physical changes by which a child's body becomes an adult body capable of reproduction.
Secular trend	A secular trend is change that occurs with respect to time.
Adolescent growth spurt	The rapid increase in weight and height that occurs around the onset of puberty is referred to as the adolescent growth spurt.
Genotype	The genotype is the specific genetic makeup of an individual, usually in the form of DNA. It codes for the phenotype of that individual. Any given gene will usually cause an observable change in an organism, known as the phenotype.
Phenotype	The phenotype of an individual organism is either its total physical appearance and constitution, or a specific manifestation of a trait, such as size or eye color, that varies between individuals. Phenotype is determined to some extent by genotype, or by the identity of the alleles that an individual carries at one or more positions on the chromosomes.
Variability	Statistically, variability refers to how much the scores in a distribution spread out, away from the mean.
Variable	A variable refers to a measurable factor, characteristic, or attribute of an individual or a system.
Accommodation	Piaget's developmental process of accommodation is the modification of currently held schemes or new schemes so that new information inconsistent with the existing schemes can be integrated and understood.
Chronological age	Chronological age refers to the number of years that have elapsed since a person's birth.
Menarche	Menarche is the first menstrual period as a girl's body progresses through the changes of puberty. Menarche usually occurs about two years after the first changes of breast development.
Early-maturing	Early-maturing girls tend to be more likely than their peers to engage in a number of deviant behaviors, such as being truant from school, getting drunk, and stealing.
Statistics	Statistics is a type of data analysis which practice includes the planning, summarizing, and interpreting of observations of a system possibly followed by predicting or forecasting of future events based on a mathematical model of the system being observed.
Statistic	A statistic is an observable random variable of a sample.
Steroid	A steroid is a lipid characterized by a carbon skeleton with four fused rings. Different steroids vary in the functional groups attached to these rings. Hundreds of distinct steroids have been identified in plants and animals. Their most important role in most living systems is as hormones.
Corticosteroid	The Corticosteroid is a class of steroid hormones that are produced in the adrenal cortex. They are involved in a wide range of physiologic systems such as stress response, immune response and regulation of inflammation, carbohydrate metabolism, protein catabolism, blood electrolyte levels, and behavior.
Affect	A subjective feeling or emotional tone often accompanied by bodily expressions noticeable to others is called affect.

112

Go to **Cram101.com** for the Practice Tests for this Chapter.

Motility	Motility is the ability to move spontaneously and independently. The term can apply to single cells, or to multicellular organisms.
Socioeconomic	Socioeconomic pertains to the study of the social and economic impacts of any product or service offering, market intervention or other activity on an economy as a whole and on the companies, organization and individuals who are its main economic actors.
Consciousness	The awareness of the sensations, thoughts, and feelings being experienced at a given moment is called consciousness.
Obsession	An obsession is a thought or idea that the sufferer cannot stop thinking about. Common examples include fears of acquiring disease, getting hurt, or causing harm to someone. They are typically automatic, frequent, distressing, and difficult to control or put an end to by themselves.
Lungs	The lungs are the essential organs of respiration. Its principal function is to transport oxygen from the atmosphere into the bloodstream, and excrete carbon dioxide from the bloodstream into the atmosphere.
Late adolescence	Late adolescence refers to approximately the latter half of the second decade of life. Career interests, dating, and identity exploration are often more pronounced in late adolescence than in early adolescence.
Population	Population refers to all members of a well-defined group of organisms, events, or things.
Pubescence	The two-year span preceding puberty during which the changes leading to physical and sexual maturity take place is referred to as pubescence.
Sperling	Sperling has studied cognitive psychology and was a prominent researcher in memory. He is responsible for the concept of iconic memory.
Socialization	Social rules and social relations are created, communicated, and changed in verbal and nonverbal ways creating social complexity useful in identifying outsiders and intelligent breeding partners. The process of learning these skills is called socialization.
Standard deviation	In probability and statistics, the standard deviation is the most commonly used measure of statistical dispersion. Simply put, it measures how spread out the values in a data set are.
Ejaculation	Ejaculation is the process of ejecting semen from the penis, and is usually accompanied by orgasm as a result of sexual stimulation.
Semen	Semen is a fluid that contains spermatozoa. It is secreted by the gonads of males for the fertilization of female ova.
Infancy	The developmental period that extends from birth to 18 or 24 months is called infancy.
Penis	The penis is the external male copulatory organ and the external male organ of urination. In humans, the penis is homologous to the female clitoris, as it develops from the same embryonic structure. It is capable of erection for use in copulation.
Correlation	A statistical technique for determining the degree of association between two or more variables is referred to as correlation.
Genetics	Genetics is the science of genes, heredity, and the variation of organisms.
Metabolism	Metabolism is the biochemical modification of chemical compounds in living organisms and cells.
Heredity	Heredity is the transfer of characteristics from parent to offspring through their genes.
Endocrine system	The endocrine system is a control system of ductless endocrine glands that secrete chemical messengers called hormones that circulate within the body via the bloodstream to affect

Go to **Cram101.com** for the Practice Tests for this Chapter.

	distant organs. It does not include exocrine glands such as salivary glands, sweat glands and glands within the gastrointestinal tract.
Nervous system	The body's electrochemical communication circuitry, made up of billions of neurons is a nervous system.
Gonads	The gonads are the organs that make gametes. Gametes are haploid germ cells. For example, sperm and egg cells are gametes. In the male the gonads are the testicles, and in the female the gonads are the ovaries.
Pituitary gland	The pituitary gland is an endocrine gland about the size of a pea that sits in the small, bony cavity at the base of the brain. The pituitary gland secretes hormones regulating a wide variety of bodily activities, including trophic hormones that stimulate other endocrine glands.
Brain	The brain controls and coordinates most movement, behavior and homeostatic body functions such as heartbeat, blood pressure, fluid balance and body temperature. Functions of the brain are responsible for cognition, emotion, memory, motor learning and other sorts of learning. The brain is primarily made up of two types of cells: glia and neurons.
Hormone	A hormone is a chemical messenger from one cell (or group of cells) to another. The best known are those produced by endocrine glands, but they are produced by nearly every organ system. The function of hormones is to serve as a signal to the target cells; the action of the hormone is determined by the pattern of secretion and the signal transduction of the receiving tissue.
Endocrine gland	An endocrine gland is one of a set of internal organs involved in the secretion of hormones into the blood. The other major type of gland is the exocrine glands, which secrete substances—usually digestive juices—into the digestive tract or onto the skin.
Estrogen	Estrogen is a group of steroid compounds that function as the primary female sex hormone. They are produced primarily by developing follicles in the ovaries, the corpus luteum and the placenta.
Amenorrhea	Amenorrhea (AmE) is the absence of a menstrual period in a woman of reproductive age. Physiologic states of amenorrhea are seen during pregnancy and lactation (breastfeeding). Outside of the reproductive years there is absence of menses during childhood and after menopause.
Secondary sex characteristics	Secondary sex characteristics are traits that distinguish the two sexes of a species, but that are not directly part of the reproductive system.
Stages	Stages represent relatively discrete periods of time in which functioning is qualitatively different from functioning at other periods.
Clitoris	Clitoris refers to an external female sex organ that is highly sensitive to sexual stimulation.
Labia	The major and minor lips of the female genitalia are called labia.
Uterus	The uterus or womb is the major female reproductive organ. The main function of the uterus is to accept a fertilized ovum which becomes implanted into the endometrium, and derives nourishment from blood vessels which develop exclusively for this purpose.
Individual differences	Individual differences psychology studies the ways in which individual people differ in their behavior. This is distinguished from other aspects of psychology in that although psychology is ostensibly a study of individuals, modern psychologists invariably study groups.
Testes	Testes are the male reproductive glands or gonads; this is where sperm develop and are stored.

Gland	A gland is an organ in an animal's body that synthesizes a substance for release such as hormones, often into the bloodstream or into cavities inside the body or its outer surface.
Seminal fluid	Seminal fluid is produced by the prostate and other glands that carries and nourishes sperm.
Prostate	The prostate is a gland that supplies most of the fluid that makes up semen, it is located at the base of the uninary bladder.
Masturbation	Masturbation is the manual excitation of the sexual organs, most often to the point of orgasm. It can refer to excitation either by oneself or by another, but commonly refers to such activities performed alone.
Testosterone	Testosterone is a steroid hormone from the androgen group. It is the principal male sex hormone and the "original" anabolic steroid.
Nocturnal	A person who exhibits nocturnal habits is referred to as a night owl.
Scrotum	The scrotum is an external sack of skin that holds the testes.
Masters and Johnson	Masters and Johnson produced the four stage model of sexual response, which they described as the human sexual response cycle. They defined the four stages of this cycle as: excitement phase, plateau phase, orgasm, and resolution phase.
Hypothesis	A specific statement about behavior or mental processes that is testable through research is a hypothesis.

Generalization	In conditioning, the tendency for a conditioned response to be evoked by stimuli that are similar to the stimulus to which the response was conditioned is a generalization. The greater the similarity among the stimuli, the greater the probability of generalization.
Stages	Stages represent relatively discrete periods of time in which functioning is qualitatively different from functioning at other periods.
Developmental level	An individual's current state of physical, emotional, and intellectual development is called the developmental level.
Adolescence	The period of life bounded by puberty and the assumption of adult responsibilities is adolescence.
Reaction time	The amount of time required to respond to a stimulus is referred to as reaction time.
Affective	Affective is the way people react emotionally, their ability to feel another living thing's pain or joy.
Affordance	An affordance is a property of an object, or a feature of the immediate environment, that indicates how that object or feature can be interfaced with. The empty space within an open doorway, for instance, affords movement across that threshold.
Learning	Learning is a relatively permanent change in behavior that results from experience. Thus, to attribute a behavioral change to learning, the change must be relatively permanent and must result from experience.
Individual differences	Individual differences psychology studies the ways in which individual people differ in their behavior. This is distinguished from other aspects of psychology in that although psychology is ostensibly a study of individuals, modern psychologists invariably study groups.
Punishment	Punishment is the addtion of a stimulus that reduces the frequency of a response, or the removal of a stimulus that results in a reduction of the response.
Attention	Attention is the cognitive process of selectively concentrating on one thing while ignoring other things. Psychologists have labeled three types of attention: sustained attention, selective attention, and divided attention.
Discrimination	In Learning theory, discrimination refers the ability to distinguish between a conditioned stimulus and other stimuli. It can be brought about by extensive training or differential reinforcement. In social terms, it is the denial of privileges to a person or a group on the basis of prejudice.
Fixation	Fixation in abnormal psychology is the state where an individual becomes obsessed with an attachment to another human, animal or inanimate object. Fixation in vision refers to maintaining the gaze in a constant direction. .
Variable	A variable refers to a measurable factor, characteristic, or attribute of an individual or a system.
Positive feedback	When a change in a variable occurs in a system, the system responds. In the case of positive feedback the response of the system is to cause that variable to increase in the same direction.
Feedback	Feedback refers to information returned to a person about the effects a response has had.
Conditioning	Conditioning describes the process by which behaviors can be learned or modified through interaction with the environment.
Motivation	In psychology, motivation is the driving force (desire) behind all actions of an organism.
Habit	A habit is a response that has become completely separated from its eliciting stimulus. Early learning theorists used the term to describe S-R associations, however not all S-R

associations become a habit, rather many are extinguished after reinforcement is withdrawn.

Intrinsic motivation   Intrinsic motivation causes people to engage in an activity for its own sake. They are subjective factors and include self-determination, curiosity, challenge, effort, and others.

Construct   A generalized concept, such as anxiety or gravity, is a construct.

Adolescence	The period of life bounded by puberty and the assumption of adult responsibilities is adolescence.
Reliability	Reliability means the extent to which a test produces a consistent , reproducible score .
Validity	The extent to which a test measures what it is intended to measure is called validity.
Variability	Statistically, variability refers to how much the scores in a distribution spread out, away from the mean.
Socioeconomic Status	A family's socioeconomic status is based on family income, parental education level, parental occupation, and social status in the community. Those with high status often have more success in preparing their children for school because they have access to a wide range of resources.
Attention	Attention is the cognitive process of selectively concentrating on one thing while ignoring other things. Psychologists have labeled three types of attention: sustained attention, selective attention, and divided attention.
Population	Population refers to all members of a well-defined group of organisms, events, or things.
Generalization	In conditioning, the tendency for a conditioned response to be evoked by stimuli that are similar to the stimulus to which the response was conditioned is a generalization. The greater the similarity among the stimuli, the greater the probability of generalization.
Random sample	A sample drawn so that each member of a population has an equal chance of being selected to participate is referred to as a random sample.
Generalizability	The ability to extend a set of findings observed in one piece of research to other situations and groups is called generalizability.
Test battery	A group of tests and interviews given to the same individual is a test battery.
Norms	In testing, standards of test performance that permit the comparison of one person's score on the test to the scores of others who have taken the same test are referred to as norms.
Variable	A variable refers to a measurable factor, characteristic, or attribute of an individual or a system.
Puberty	Puberty refers to the process of physical changes by which a child's body becomes an adult body capable of reproduction.
Early adulthood	The developmental period beginning in the late teens or early twenties and lasting into the thirties is called early adulthood; characterized by an increasing self-awareness.
Motivation	In psychology, motivation is the driving force (desire) behind all actions of an organism.
Variance	The degree to which scores differ among individuals in a distribution of scores is the variance.
Body mass index	The body mass index is a calculated number, used to compare and analyse the health effects of body weight on human bodies of all heights. It is equal to the weight, divided by the square of the height.
Statistics	Statistics is a type of data analysis which practice includes the planning, summarizing, and interpreting of observations of a system possibly followed by predicting or forecasting of future events based on a mathematical model of the system being observed.
Statistic	A statistic is an observable random variable of a sample.
Chronic	Chronic refers to a relatively long duration, usually more than a few months.
Longitudinal	Longitudinal study refers to a type of developmental study in which the same group of

study	participants is followed and measured at different ages on some set of behaviors.
Quantitative change	Quantitative change refers to change in number or amount, such as in height, weight, or size of vocabulary.
Gross motor skills	Gross motor skills refer to motor skills that involve large muscle activities, such as walking.
Secular trend	A secular trend is change that occurs with respect to time.
Middle and late childhood	Middle and late childhood refers to the developmental period extending from about 6 to about 10 or 11 years of age. During the period, children grow an average of 2 to 3 inches a year and gain about 5 to 7 pounds a year. Slow consistent growth. Head circumference, waist circumference, and leg length decrease in relation to body height. Motor movements become smoother, more coordinated.
Androgen	Androgen is the generic term for any natural or synthetic compound, usually a steroid hormone, that stimulates or controls the development and maintenance of masculine characteristics in vertebrates by binding to androgen receptors.
Gender difference	A gender difference is a disparity between genders involving quality or quantity. Though some gender differences are controversial, they are not to be confused with sexist stereotypes.
Conditioning	Conditioning describes the process by which behaviors can be learned or modified through interaction with the environment.

Go to **Cram101.com** for the Practice Tests for this Chapter.

Adolescence	The period of life bounded by puberty and the assumption of adult responsibilities is adolescence.
Society	The social sciences use the term society to mean a group of people that form a semi-closed (or semi-open) social system, in which most interactions are with other individuals belonging to the group.
Obedience	Obedience is the willingness to follow the will of others. Humans have been shown to be surprisingly obedient in the presence of perceived legitimate authority figures, as demonstrated by the Milgram experiment in the 1960s.
Role model	A person who serves as a positive example of desirable behavior is referred to as a role model.
Socialization	Social rules and social relations are created, communicated, and changed in verbal and nonverbal ways creating social complexity useful in identifying outsiders and intelligent breeding partners. The process of learning these skills is called socialization.
Attitude	An enduring mental representation of a person, place, or thing that evokes an emotional response and related behavior is called attitude.
Social role	Social role refers to expected behavior patterns associated with particular social positions.
Norms	In testing, standards of test performance that permit the comparison of one person's score on the test to the scores of others who have taken the same test are referred to as norms.
Variable	A variable refers to a measurable factor, characteristic, or attribute of an individual or a system.
Internalization	The developmental change from behavior that is externally controlled to behavior that is controlled by internal standards and principles is referred to as internalization.
Social development	The person's developing capacity for social relationships and the effects of those relationships on further development is referred to as social development.
Autonomy	Autonomy is the condition of something that does not depend on anything else.
Socioeconomic Status	A family's socioeconomic status is based on family income, parental education level, parental occupation, and social status in the community. Those with high status often have more success in preparing their children for school because they have access to a wide range of resources.
Affect	A subjective feeling or emotional tone often accompanied by bodily expressions noticeable to others is called affect.
Maturation	The orderly unfolding of traits, as regulated by the genetic code is called maturation.
Learning	Learning is a relatively permanent change in behavior that results from experience. Thus, to attribute a behavioral change to learning, the change must be relatively permanent and must result from experience.
Sexually Transmitted Disease	Sexually transmitted disease is commonly transmitted between partners through some form of sexual activity, most commonly vaginal intercourse, oral sex, or anal sex.
Suicide	Suicide behavior is rare in childhood but escalates in adolescence. The suicide rate increases in a linear fashion from adolescence through late adulthood.
Moral development	Development regarding rules and conventions about what people should do in their interactions with other people is called moral development.
Self-esteem	Self-esteem refers to a person's subjective appraisal of himself or herself as intrinsically

Go to **Cram101.com** for the Practice Tests for this Chapter.

positive or negative to some degree.

Need for Affiliation	Need for Affiliation is a term introduced by David McClelland to describe a person's need to feel like he needs to belong to a group. These individuals require warm interpersonal relationships and approval from those in these relationships is very satisfying. People who value affiliation a lot tend to be good team members, but poor leaders.
Friendship	The essentials of friendship are reciprocity and commitment between individuals who see themselves more or less as equals. Interaction between friends rests on a more equal power base than the interaction between children and adults.
Questionnaire	A self-report method of data collection or clinical assessment method in which the individual being studied checks off items on a printed list, answers multiple-choice questions, or writes out answers to essay questions aimed at producing a selfdescription is called questionnaire.
Survey	A method of scientific investigation in which a large sample of people answer questions about their attitudes or behavior is referred to as a survey.
Self-concept	Self-concept refers to domain-specific evaluations of the self where a domain may be academics, athletics, etc.
Action component	How one tends to act toward the object of an attitude is called the action component.
Affective	Affective is the way people react emotionally, their ability to feel another living thing's pain or joy.
Emotion	An emotion is a mental states that arise spontaneously, rather than through conscious effort. They are often accompanied by physiological changes.
Construct	A generalized concept, such as anxiety or gravity, is a construct.
Longitudinal studies	Investigation that collects information on the same individuals repeatedly over time, perhaps over many years, in an effort to determine how phenomena change is referred to as longitudinal studies. These studies to to be time consuming and expensive.
Moral reasoning	Moral reasoning involves concepts of justice, whereas social conventional judgments are concepts of social organization.
Kohlberg	Kohlberg believed that people progressed in their moral reasoning through a series of developmental stages.
Stages	Stages represent relatively discrete periods of time in which functioning is qualitatively different from functioning at other periods.
Preconventional level	According to Kohlberg, the preconventional level is a period during which moral judgments are based largely on expectation of rewards or punishments.
Punishment	Punishment is the addtion of a stimulus that reduces the frequency of a response, or the removal of a stimulus that results in a reduction of the response.
Conventional level	According to Kohlberg, a period during which moral judgments is largely reflective of social conventions is the conventional level. It is a "law and order" approach to morality.
Postconventional morality	The third level in Kohlberg's theory of moral reasoning, postconventional morality, suggests individuals can follow internally held moral principles and are able to decide among conflicting moral standards.
Cognitive dissonance	Cognitive dissonance is a state of opposition between cognitions. Contradicting cognitions serve as a driving force that compel the mind to acquire or invent new thoughts or beliefs, or to modify existing beliefs, so as to minimize the amount of dissonance between cognitions.

Go to **Cram101.com** for the Practice Tests for this Chapter.

Moral education	Three types of moral education are character education, values clarification, and cognitive moral education.

Projection	Attributing one's own undesirable thoughts, impulses, traits, or behaviors to others is referred to as projection.
Population	Population refers to all members of a well-defined group of organisms, events, or things.
Affective	Affective is the way people react emotionally, their ability to feel another living thing's pain or joy.
Affect	A subjective feeling or emotional tone often accompanied by bodily expressions noticeable to others is called affect.
Middle Adulthood	Middle adulthood refers to the developmental period beginning at approximately 40 years of age and extending to about 60. Maximum bone density occurs by the late thirties and begins to degrade.
Adolescence	The period of life bounded by puberty and the assumption of adult responsibilities is adolescence.
Life span	Life span refers to the upper boundary of life, the maximum number of years an individual can live. The maximum life span of human beings is about 120 years of age. Females live an average of 6 years longer than males.
Infancy	The developmental period that extends from birth to 18 or 24 months is called infancy.
Variability	Statistically, variability refers to how much the scores in a distribution spread out, away from the mean.
Brain	The brain controls and coordinates most movement, behavior and homeostatic body functions such as heartbeat, blood pressure, fluid balance and body temperature. Functions of the brain are responsible for cognition, emotion, memory, motor learning and other sorts of learning. The brain is primarily made up of two types of cells: glia and neurons.
Motivation	In psychology, motivation is the driving force (desire) behind all actions of an organism.
Genetics	Genetics is the science of genes, heredity, and the variation of organisms.
Variable	A variable refers to a measurable factor, characteristic, or attribute of an individual or a system.
Theories	Theories are logically self-consistent models or frameworks describing the behavior of a certain natural or social phenomenon. They are broad explanations and predictions concerning phenomena of interest.
Maturation	The orderly unfolding of traits, as regulated by the genetic code is called maturation.
Mutation	Mutation is a permanent, sometimes transmissible (if the change is to a germ cell) change to the genetic material (usually DNA or RNA) of a cell. They can be caused by copying errors in the genetic material during cell division and by exposure to radiation, chemicals, or viruses, or can occur deliberately under cellular control during the processes such as meiosis or hypermutation.
Immune system	The most important function of the human immune system occurs at the cellular level of the blood and tissues. The lymphatic and blood circulation systems are highways for specialized white blood cells. These cells include B cells, T cells, natural killer cells, and macrophages. All function with the primary objective of recognizing, attacking and destroying bacteria, viruses, cancer cells, and all substances seen as foreign.
Spleen	The spleen is a ductless gland that is not necessary for life but is closely associated with the circulatory system, where it functions in the destruction of old red blood cells and removal of other debris from the bloodstream, and also in holding a reservoir of blood.
Homeostasis	Homeostasis is the property of an open system, especially living organisms, to regulate its

Go to **Cram101.com** for the Practice Tests for this Chapter.

	internal environment so as to maintain a stable condition, by means of multiple dynamic equilibrium adjustments controlled by interrelated regulation mechanisms.
Life expectancy	The number of years that will probably be lived by the average person born in a particular year is called life expectancy.
Cholesterol	Cholesterol is a steroid, a lipid, and an alcohol, found in the cell membranes of all body tissues, and transported in the blood plasma of all animals. Cholesterol is an important component of the membranes of cells, providing stability; it makes the membrane's fluidity stable over a bigger temperature interval.
Antioxidants	Antioxidants are chemicals that prevent the oxidation of other chemicals. The normal processes of oxidation produce highly reactive free radicals. These can readily react with and damage other molecules. The presence of extremely easily oxidisable compounds in the system can "mop up" free radicals before they damage other essential molecules.
Physiological changes	Alterations in heart rate, blood pressure, perspiration, and other involuntary responses are physiological changes.
Central nervous system	The vertebrate central nervous system consists of the brain and spinal cord.
Skeletal muscle	Skeletal muscle is a type of striated muscle, attached to the skeleton. They are used to facilitate movement, by applying force to bones and joints; via contraction. They generally contract voluntarily (via nerve stimulation), although they can contract involuntarily.
Osteoporosis	Osteoporosis refers to a disorder of aging that involves an extensive loss of bone tissue and is the main reason many older adults walk with a marked stoop. Women are especially vulnerable to osteoporosis.
Endocrine system	The endocrine system is a control system of ductless endocrine glands that secrete chemical messengers called hormones that circulate within the body via the bloodstream to affect distant organs. It does not include exocrine glands such as salivary glands, sweat glands and glands within the gastrointestinal tract.
Metabolism	Metabolism is the biochemical modification of chemical compounds in living organisms and cells.
Viscera	The internal organs of the body are called viscera.
Menopause	Menopause is a stage of the human female reproductive cycle that occurs as the ovaries stop producing estrogen, causing the reproductive system to gradually shut down.
Early adulthood	The developmental period beginning in the late teens or early twenties and lasting into the thirties is called early adulthood; characterized by an increasing self-awareness.
Arthritis	Arthritis is a group of conditions that affect the health of the bone joints in the body. Arthritis can be caused from strains and injuries caused by repetitive motion, sports, overexertion, and falls. Unlike the autoimmune diseases, it largely affects older people and results from the degeneration of joint cartilage.
Spinal cord	The spinal cord is a part of the vertebrate nervous system that is enclosed in and protected by the vertebral column (it passes through the spinal canal). It consists of nerve cells. The spinal cord carries sensory signals and motor innervation to most of the skeletal muscles in the body.
Neuron	The neuron is the primary cell of the nervous system. They are found in the brain, the spinal cord, in the nerves and ganglia of the peripheral nervous system. It is a specialized cell that conducts impulses through the nervous system and contains three major parts: cell body, dendrites, and an axon. It can have many dendrites but only one axon.

Dendrite	A dendrite is a slender, typically branched projection of a nerve cell, or "neuron," which conducts the electrical stimulation received from other cells to the body or soma of the cell from which it projects. This stimulation arrives through synapses, which typically are located near the tips of the dendrites and away from the soma.
Axon	An axon, or "nerve fiber," is a long slender projection of a nerve cell, or "neuron," which conducts electrical impulses away from the neuron's cell body or soma.
Neurotransmitter	A neurotransmitter is a chemical that is used to relay, amplify and modulate electrical signals between a neurons and another cell.
Cerebral cortex	The cerebral cortex is the outermost layer of the cerebrum and has a grey color. It is made up of four lobes and it is involved in many complex brain functions including memory, perceptual awareness, "thinking", language and consciousness. The cerebral cortex receives sensory information from many different sensory organs eg: eyes, ears, etc. and processes the information.
Compensation	In personaility, compensation, according to Adler, is an effort to overcome imagined or real inferiorities by developing one's abilities.
Plasticity	The capacity for modification and change is referred to as plasticity.
Neurofibrillary tangles	Neurofibrillary tangles are pathological protein aggregates found within neurons in cases of Alzheimer's disease.
Senile plaques	Senile plaques are clumps of A-beta peptides commonly found in Alzheimer's disease on microscopic examination of brain tissue.
Plaques	Plaques refer to small, round areas composed of remnants of lost neurons and beta-amyloid, a waxy protein deposit; present in the brains of patients with Alzheimer's disease.
Synapse	A synapse is specialized junction through which cells of the nervous system signal to one another and to non-neuronal cells such as muscles or glands.
Dopamine	Dopamine is critical to the way the brain controls our movements and is a crucial part of the basal ganglia motor loop. It is commonly associated with the 'pleasure system' of the brain, providing feelings of enjoyment and reinforcement to motivate us to do, or continue doing, certain activities.
Nerve	A nerve is an enclosed, cable-like bundle of nerve fibers or axons, which includes the glia that ensheath the axons in myelin. Neurons are sometimes called nerve cells, though this term is technically imprecise since many neurons do not form nerves.
Larynx	The larynx, or voicebox, is an organ in the neck of mammals involved in protection of the trachea and sound production. The larynx houses the vocal cords, and is situated at the point where the upper tract splits into the trachea and the esophagus.
Lungs	The lungs are the essential organs of respiration. Its principal function is to transport oxygen from the atmosphere into the bloodstream, and excrete carbon dioxide from the bloodstream into the atmosphere.
Liver	The liver plays a major role in metabolism and has a number of functions in the body including detoxification, glycogen storage and plasma protein synthesis. It also produces bile, which is important for digestion. The liver converts most carbohydrates, proteing, and fats into glucose.
Physiology	The study of the functions and activities of living cells, tissues, and organs and of the physical and chemical phenomena involved is referred to as physiology.
Anatomy	Anatomy is the branch of biology that deals with the structure and organization of living things. It can be divided into animal anatomy (zootomy) and plant anatomy (phytonomy). Major

Go to **Cram101.com** for the Practice Tests for this Chapter.

branches of anatomy include comparative anatomy, histology, and human anatomy.

Collagen	Collagen is the main protein of connective tissue in animals and the most abundant protein in mammals, making up about 1/4 of the total. It is one of the long, fibrous structural proteins whose functions are quite different from those of globular proteins such as enzymes.
Cardiovascular disease	Cardiovascular disease refers to afflictions in the mechanisms, including the heart, blood vessels, and their controllers, that are responsible for transporting blood to the body's tissues and organs. Psychological factors may play important roles in such diseases and their treatments.
Atherosclerosis	Process by which a fatty substance or plaque builds up inside arteries to form obstructions is called atherosclerosis.
Coronary heart disease	Coronary heart disease is the end result of the accumulation of atheromatous plaques within the walls of the arteries that supply the myocardium (the muscle of the heart).
Aerobic exercise	Aerobic exercise is a type of exercise in which muscles draw on oxygen in the blood as well as fats and glucose, that increase cardiovascular endurance.
Hypertension	Hypertension is a medical condition where the blood pressure in the arteries is chronically elevated. Persistent hypertension is one of the risk factors for strokes, heart attacks, heart failure and arterial aneurysm, and is a leading cause of chronic renal failure.
Depression	In everyday language depression refers to any downturn in mood, which may be relatively transitory and perhaps due to something trivial. This is differentiated from Clinical depression which is marked by symptoms that last two weeks or more and are so severe that they interfere with daily living.
Diabetes	Diabetes is a medical disorder characterized by varying or persistent elevated blood sugar levels, especially after eating. All types of diabetes share similar symptoms and complications at advanced stages: dehydration and ketoacidosis, cardiovascular disease, chronic renal failure, retinal damage which can lead to blindness, nerve damage which can lead to erectile dysfunction, gangrene with risk of amputation of toes, feet, and even legs.
Chronic	Chronic refers to a relatively long duration, usually more than a few months.
Sensory receptor	A sensory receptor is a structure that recognizes a stimulus in the environment of an organism. In response to stimuli the sensory receptor initiates sensory transduction by creating graded potentials or action potentials in the same cell or in an adjacent one.
Sensation	Sensation is the first stage in the chain of biochemical and neurologic events that begins with the impinging of a stimulus upon the receptor cells of a sensory organ, which then leads to perception, the mental state that is reflected in statements like "I see a uniformly blue wall."
Proprioception	Proprioception is the sense of the position of parts of the body, relative to other neighboring parts of the body.
Vitreous humor	Vitreous humor is the clear aqueous solution that fills the space between the lens and the retina of the vertebrate eyeball. The primary purpose to provide a cushioned support for the rest of the eye, as well as a clear unobstructed path for light to travel to the retina.
Aqueous humor	The aqueous humor is the clear, watery fluid that fills the complex space in the front of the eye which is bounded at the front by the cornea and at the rear by the front surface or face of the vitreous humor.
Retina	The retina is a thin layer of cells at the back of the eyeball. It is the part of the eye which converts light into nervous signals. The retina contains photoreceptor cells which receive the light; the resulting neural signals then undergo complex processing by other

neurons of the retina, and are transformed into action potentials in retinal ganglion cells whose axons form the optic nerve.

Cornea	The cornea is the transparent front part of the eye that covers the iris, pupil, and anterior chamber and provides most of an eye's optical power. Together with the lens, the cornea refracts light and consequently helps the eye to focus.
Pupil	In the eye, the pupil is the opening in the middle of the iris. It appears black because most of the light entering it is absorbed by the tissues inside the eye. The size of the pupil is controlled by involuntary contraction and dilation of the iris, in order to regulate the intensity of light entering the eye. This is known as the pupillary reflex.
Iris	The iris is the most visible part of the eye. The iris is an annulus (or flattened ring) consisting of pigmented fibrovascular tissue known as a stroma. The stroma connects a sphincter muscle, which contracts the pupil, and a set of dialator muscles which open it.
Crystalline lens	The crystalline lens is a transparent, biconvex structure in the eye that, along with the cornea, helps to refract light to focus on the retina. The lens is flexible and its curvature is controlled by ciliary muscles. By changing the curvature of the lens, one can focus the eye on objects at different distances from it. This process is called accommodation.
Optic nerve	The optic nerve is the nerve that transmits visual information from the retina to the brain. The optic nerve is composed of retinal ganglion cell axons and support cells.
Cataracts	A cataract is any opacity which develops in the crystalline lens of the eye or in its envelope. Cataracts form for a variety of reasons, including long term ultraviolet exposure, secondary effects of diseases such as diabetes, or simply due to advanced age.
Receptor	A sensory receptor is a structure that recognizes a stimulus in the internal or external environment of an organism. In response to stimuli the sensory receptor initiates sensory transduction by creating graded potentials or action potentials in the same cell or in an adjacent one.
Auditory system	The auditory system is the sensory system for the sense of hearing. On its path from the outside world to the forebrain, sound information is preserved and modified in many ways. It changes media twice, first from air to fluid, then from fluid to action potentials.
Feedback	Feedback refers to information returned to a person about the effects a response has had.
Outer ear	Outer ear consists of the pinna and the external auditory canal.
Pinna	The pinna is the visible part of the ear that resides outside of the head. It acts as a funnel, amplifying the sound and directing it to the ear canal. While reflecting from the pinna, sound also goes through a filtering process which adds directional information to the sound.
Tympanic membrane	The tympanic membrane, colloquially known as eardrum, is a thin membrane that separates the outer ear from the middle ear. Its function is to transmit sound from the air to the ossicles inside the middle ear.
Organ of Corti	The Organ of Corti is the hearing organ of the inner ear. It contains receptors that respond to vibrations in the basilar membrane which are caused by sound.
Inner ear	The inner ear consists of the oval window, cochlea, and basilar membrane.
Auditory nerve	The vestibulocochlear nerve is the eighth of twelve cranial nerves, and also known as the auditory nerve. It is the nerve along which the sensory cells (the hair cells) of the inner ear transmit information to the brain. It consists of the cochlear nerve, carrying information about hearing, and the vestibular nerve, carrying information about balance.
Vestibular	The vestibular system, or balance system, is the sensory system that provides the dominant

system	input about our movement and orientation in space. Together with the cochlea, the auditory organ, it is situated in the vestibulum in the inner ear.
Semicircular canals	The semicircular canals are three half-circular, interconnected tubes located inside each ear that are the equivalent of three gyroscopes located in three planes perpendicular (at right angles) to each other.
Endolymph	Endolymph is the fluid contained in the membranous labyrinth of the inner ear. Disruption of the endolymph due to jerky movements (like driving over bumps while riding in a car) can cause motion sickness.
Malleus	The malleus is hammer-shaped small bone or ossicle of the middle ear which connects with the incus and is attached to the inner surface of the eardrum.
Hair cells	Hair cells are the sensory cells of both the auditory system and the vestibular system. The auditory hair cells are located within the organ of Corti on a thin basilar membrane in the cochlea of the inner ear.
Habit	A habit is a response that has become completely separated from its eliciting stimulus. Early learning theorists used the term to describe S-R associations, however not all S-R associations become a habit, rather many are extinguished after reinforcement is withdrawn.

Go to **Cram101.com** for the Practice Tests for this Chapter.

Variability	Statistically, variability refers to how much the scores in a distribution spread out, away from the mean.
Variable	A variable refers to a measurable factor, characteristic, or attribute of an individual or a system.
Compensation	In personaility, compensation, according to Adler, is an effort to overcome imagined or real inferiorities by developing one's abilities.
Central nervous system	The vertebrate central nervous system consists of the brain and spinal cord.
Affect	A subjective feeling or emotional tone often accompanied by bodily expressions noticeable to others is called affect.
Reaction time	The amount of time required to respond to a stimulus is referred to as reaction time.
Stimulus	A change in an environmental condition that elicits a response is a stimulus.
Insight	Insight refers to a sudden awareness of the relationships among various elements that had previously appeared to be independent of one another.
Electromyography	Electromyography is a medical technique for measuring muscle response to nervous stimulation.
Brain	The brain controls and coordinates most movement, behavior and homeostatic body functions such as heartbeat, blood pressure, fluid balance and body temperature. Functions of the brain are responsible for cognition, emotion, memory, motor learning and other sorts of learning. The brain is primarily made up of two types of cells: glia and neurons.
Motor cortex	Motor cortex refers to the section of cortex that lies in the frontal lobe, just across the central fissure from the sensory cortex. Neural impulses in the motor cortex are linked to muscular responses throughout the body.
Middle Adulthood	Middle adulthood refers to the developmental period beginning at approximately 40 years of age and extending to about 60. Maximum bone density occurs by the late thirties and begins to degrade.
Auditory system	The auditory system is the sensory system for the sense of hearing. On its path from the outside world to the forebrain, sound information is preserved and modified in many ways. It changes media twice, first from air to fluid, then from fluid to action potentials.
Motivation	In psychology, motivation is the driving force (desire) behind all actions of an organism.
Depression	In everyday language depression refers to any downturn in mood, which may be relatively transitory and perhaps due to something trivial. This is differentiated from Clinical depression which is marked by symptoms that last two weeks or more and are so severe that they interfere with daily living.
Anxiety	Anxiety is a complex combination of the feeling of fear, apprehension and worry often accompanied by physical sensations such as palpitations, chest pain and/or shortness of breath.
Amplitude	Amplitude is a nonnegative scalar measure of a wave's magnitude of oscillation.
Neurotransmitter	A neurotransmitter is a chemical that is used to relay, amplify and modulate electrical signals between a neurons and another cell.
Nerve	A nerve is an enclosed, cable-like bundle of nerve fibers or axons, which includes the glia that ensheath the axons in myelin. Neurons are sometimes called nerve cells, though this term is technically imprecise since many neurons do not form nerves.
Somatosensory	Somatosensory system consists of the various sensory receptors that trigger the experiences

Go to **Cram101.com** for the Practice Tests for this Chapter.

system	labelled as touch or pressure, temperature, pain, and the sensations of muscle movement and joint position including posture, movement, and facial expression.
Agonist	Agonist refers to a drug that mimics or increases a neurotransmitter's effects.
Receptor	A sensory receptor is a structure that recognizes a stimulus in the internal or external environment of an organism. In response to stimuli the sensory receptor initiates sensory transduction by creating graded potentials or action potentials in the same cell or in an adjacent one.
Retina	The retina is a thin layer of cells at the back of the eyeball. It is the part of the eye which converts light into nervous signals. The retina contains photoreceptor cells which receive the light; the resulting neural signals then undergo complex processing by other neurons of the retina, and are transformed into action potentials in retinal ganglion cells whose axons form the optic nerve.
Contusion	Brain contusion, a form of traumatic brain injury, is a bruise of the brain tissue. Like bruises in other tissues, cerebral contusion can be caused by multiple microhemorrhages, small blood vessel leaks into brain tissue.
Osteoporosis	Osteoporosis refers to a disorder of aging that involves an extensive loss of bone tissue and is the main reason many older adults walk with a marked stoop. Women are especially vulnerable to osteoporosis.
Feedback	Feedback refers to information returned to a person about the effects a response has had.
Vestibular system	The vestibular system, or balance system, is the sensory system that provides the dominant input about our movement and orientation in space. Together with the cochlea, the auditory organ, it is situated in the vestibulum in the inner ear.
Stroke	A stroke occurs when the blood supply to a part of the brain is suddenly interrupted by occlusion, by hemorrhage, or other causes
Arthritis	Arthritis is a group of conditions that affect the health of the bone joints in the body. Arthritis can be caused from strains and injuries caused by repetitive motion, sports, overexertion, and falls. Unlike the autoimmune diseases, it largely affects older people and results from the degeneration of joint cartilage.
Drug interaction	A combined effect of two drugs that exceeds the addition of one drug's effects to the other is a drug interaction.
Antidepressants	Antidepressants are medications used primarily in the treatment of clinical depression. Antidepressants create little if any immediate change in mood and require between several days and several weeks to take effect.
Antidepressant	An antidepressant is a medication used primarily in the treatment of clinical depression. They are not thought to produce tolerance, although sudden withdrawal may produce adverse effects. They create little if any immediate change in mood and require between several days and several weeks to take effect.
Sedative	A sedative is a drug that depresses the central nervous system (CNS), which causes calmness, relaxation, reduction of anxiety, sleepiness, slowed breathing, slurred speech, staggering gait, poor judgment, and slow, uncertain reflexes.
Visual perception	Visual perception is one of the senses, consisting of the ability to detect light and interpret it. Vision has a specific sensory system.
Multiple sclerosis	Multiple sclerosis affects neurons, the cells of the brain and spinal cord that carry information, create thought and perception, and allow the brain to control the body. Surrounding and protecting these neurons is a layer of fat, called myelin, which helps

Go to **Cram101.com** for the Practice Tests for this Chapter.

	neurons carry electrical signals. MS causes gradual destruction of myelin (demyelination) in patches throughout the brain and/or spinal cord, causing various symptoms depending upon which signals are interrupted.
Tumor	A tumor is an abnormal growth that when located in the brain can either be malignant and directly destroy brain tissue, or be benign and disrupt functioning by increasing intracranial pressure.
Attention	Attention is the cognitive process of selectively concentrating on one thing while ignoring other things. Psychologists have labeled three types of attention: sustained attention, selective attention, and divided attention.
Acquisition	Acquisition is the process of adapting to the environment, learning or becoming conditioned. In classical conditoning terms, it is the initial learning of the stimulus response link, which involves a neutral stimulus being associated with a unconditioned stimulus and becoming a conditioned stimulus.
Learning	Learning is a relatively permanent change in behavior that results from experience. Thus, to attribute a behavioral change to learning, the change must be relatively permanent and must result from experience.
Population	Population refers to all members of a well-defined group of organisms, events, or things.

150

Go to **Cram101.com** for the Practice Tests for this Chapter.

Self-concept	Self-concept refers to domain-specific evaluations of the self where a domain may be academics, athletics, etc.
Affect	A subjective feeling or emotional tone often accompanied by bodily expressions noticeable to others is called affect.
Self-esteem	Self-esteem refers to a person's subjective appraisal of himself or herself as intrinsically positive or negative to some degree.
Body image	A person's body image is their perception of their physical appearance. It is more than what a person thinks they will see in a mirror, it is inextricably tied to their self-esteem and acceptance by peers.
Locus of control	The place to which an individual attributes control over the receiving of reinforcers -either inside or outside the self is referred to as locus of control.
Perception	Perception is the process of acquiring, interpreting, selecting, and organizing sensory information.
Depression	In everyday language depression refers to any downturn in mood, which may be relatively transitory and perhaps due to something trivial. This is differentiated from Clinical depression which is marked by symptoms that last two weeks or more and are so severe that they interfere with daily living.
Socialization	Social rules and social relations are created, communicated, and changed in verbal and nonverbal ways creating social complexity useful in identifying outsiders and intelligent breeding partners. The process of learning these skills is called socialization.
Ageism	Ageism is bias against a person or group on the grounds of age. When that bias is the primary motivation behind acts of discrimination against that person or group, then those acts constitute age discrimination..
Stages	Stages represent relatively discrete periods of time in which functioning is qualitatively different from functioning at other periods.
Late adulthood	The developmental period that lasts from about 60 to 70 years of age until death is referred to as late adulthood.
Generativity	Generativity refers to an adult's concern for and commitment to the well-being of future generations.
Intimacy versus isolation	The life crisis of young adulthood, which is characterized by the task of developing binding intimate relationships is referred to as Erikson's intimacy versus isolation stage.
Early adulthood	The developmental period beginning in the late teens or early twenties and lasting into the thirties is called early adulthood; characterized by an increasing self-awareness.
Friendship	The essentials of friendship are reciprocity and commitment between individuals who see themselves more or less as equals. Interaction between friends rests on a more equal power base than the interaction between children and adults.
Generativity versus stagnation	Generativity versus stagnation is Erikson's term for the crisis of middle adulthood. The individual is characterized by the task of being productive and contributing to younger generations.
Middle Adulthood	Middle adulthood refers to the developmental period beginning at approximately 40 years of age and extending to about 60. Maximum bone density occurs by the late thirties and begins to degrade.
Society	The social sciences use the term society to mean a group of people that form a semi-closed (or semi-open) social system, in which most interactions are with other individuals belonging

	to the group.
Midlife crisis	Midlife crisis refers to a period of turmoil usually occurring in a person's 40s and brought on by an awareness of one's mortality; characterized by a reassessment of one's life and a decision to make changes, either drastic or moderate, in order to make the remaining years better.
Integrity versus despair	Erikson's eighth and final stage of development is Integrity Versus Despair. In late adulthood individuals reflect on the past and either piece together a positive review or conclude that one's life has not been well spent.
Life structure	Life structure is Daniel Levinson's term for the basic pattern of one's life at any given time, including one's relationships and activities and the significance they have for the individual.
Insight	Insight refers to a sudden awareness of the relationships among various elements that had previously appeared to be independent of one another.
Socioeconomic	Socioeconomic pertains to the study of the social and economic impacts of any product or service offering, market intervention or other activity on an economy as a whole and on the companies, organization and individuals who are its main economic actors.
Adolescence	The period of life bounded by puberty and the assumption of adult responsibilities is adolescence.
Midlife transition	Levinson's term for the ages from 40 to 45, which are characterized by a shift in psychological perspective from viewing ourselves in terms of years lived to viewing ourselves in terms of the years we have left is called the midlife transition.
Individualism	Individualism refers to putting personal goals ahead of group goals and defining one's identity in terms of personal attributes rather than group memberships.
Variable	A variable refers to a measurable factor, characteristic, or attribute of an individual or a system.
Attitude	An enduring mental representation of a person, place, or thing that evokes an emotional response and related behavior is called attitude.
Chronic	Chronic refers to a relatively long duration, usually more than a few months.
Population	Population refers to all members of a well-defined group of organisms, events, or things.
Menopause	Menopause is a stage of the human female reproductive cycle that occurs as the ovaries stop producing estrogen, causing the reproductive system to gradually shut down.
Clinical depression	Although nearly any mood with some element of sadness may colloquially be termed a depression, clinical depression is more than just a temporary state of sadness. Symptoms lasting two weeks or longer in duration, and of a severity that they begin to interfere with daily living.
Disengagement theory	Disengagement theory of aging suggests that aging is a gradual withdrawal from the world on physical, psychological, and social levels.
Activity theory	Activity theory states that the more active and involved older adults are, the more likely they are to be satisfied with their lives.
Theories	Theories are logically self-consistent models or frameworks describing the behavior of a certain natural or social phenomenon. They are broad explanations and predictions concerning phenomena of interest.
Denial	Denial is a psychological defense mechanism in which a person faced with a fact that is uncomfortable or painful to accept rejects it instead, insisting that it is not true despite

Go to **Cram101.com** for the Practice Tests for this Chapter.

	what may be overwhelming evidence.
Self-worth	In psychology, self-esteem or self-worth refers to a person's subjective appraisal of himself or herself as intrinsically positive or negative to some degree.
Prejudice	Prejudice in general, implies coming to a judgment on the subject before learning where the preponderance of the evidence actually lies, or formation of a judgement without direct experience.
Gerontology	Gerontology is the study of the elderly, and of the aging process itself. It is to be distinguished from geriatrics, which is the study of the diseases of the elderly. Gerontology covers the social, psychological and biology aspects of aging.
Stereotype	A stereotype is considered to be a group concept, held by one social group about another.They are often used in a negative or prejudicial sense and are frequently used to justify certain discriminatory behaviors. This allows powerful social groups to legitimize and protect their dominant position
Psychosocial development	Erikson's psychosocial development describe eight developmental stages through which a healthily developing human should pass from infancy to late adulthood. In each stage the person confronts, and hopefully masters, new challenges.
Erik Erikson	Erik Erikson conceived eight stages of development, each confronting the individual with its own psychosocial demands, that continued into old age. Personality development, according to Erikson, takes place through a series of crises that must be overcome and internalized by the individual in preparation for the next developmental stage. Such crisis are not catastrophes but vulnerabilities.

Insight	Insight refers to a sudden awareness of the relationships among various elements that had previously appeared to be independent of one another.
Reliability	Reliability means the extent to which a test produces a consistent , reproducible score .
Validity	The extent to which a test measures what it is intended to measure is called validity.
Construct validity	The extent to which there is evidence that a test measures a particular hypothetical construct is referred to as construct validity.
Content validity	The degree to which the content of a test is representative of the domain it's supposed to cover is referred to as its content validity.
Population	Population refers to all members of a well-defined group of organisms, events, or things.
Test norms	Test norms are standards that provide information about where a score on a psychological test ranks in relation to other scores on that test .
Norms	In testing, standards of test performance that permit the comparison of one person's score on the test to the scores of others who have taken the same test are referred to as norms.
Quantitative	A quantitative property is one that exists in a range of magnitudes, and can therefore be measured. Measurements of any particular quantitative property are expressed as as a specific quantity, referred to as a unit, multiplied by a number.
Attention	Attention is the cognitive process of selectively concentrating on one thing while ignoring other things. Psychologists have labeled three types of attention: sustained attention, selective attention, and divided attention.
Stroke	A stroke occurs when the blood supply to a part of the brain is suddenly interrupted by occlusion, by hemorrhage, or other causes
Toddler	A toddler is a child between the ages of one and three years old. During this period, the child learns a great deal about social roles and develops motor skills; to toddle is to walk unsteadily.
Early childhood	Early childhood refers to the developmental period extending from the end of infancy to about 5 or 6 years of age; sometimes called the preschool years.
Infancy	The developmental period that extends from birth to 18 or 24 months is called infancy.
Infant mortality	Infant mortality is the death of infants in the first year of life. The leading causes of infant mortality are dehydration and disease. Major causes of infant mortality in more developed countries include congenital malformation, infection and SIDS. Infant mortality rate is the number of newborns dying under a year of age divided by the number of live births during the year.
Apgar score	The Apgar score was devised in 1952 by Virginia Apgar as a simple and repeatable method to quickly and summarily assess the health of newborn children immediately after childbirth.
Standardized test	An oral or written assessment for which an individual receives a score indicating how the individual reponded relative to a previously tested large sample of others is referred to as a standardized test.
Developmental level	An individual's current state of physical, emotional, and intellectual development is called the developmental level.
Bayley Scales	The Bayley Scales of Infant Development are widely used in assessing infant development for infants 1-42 months of age. The current version has three parts: a Mental Scale, a Motor Scale, and the Infant Behavior Profile. Among the uses are the diagnosis of developmental delays and the planning of intervention strategies.

Go to **Cram101.com** for the Practice Tests for this Chapter.

Adolescence	The period of life bounded by puberty and the assumption of adult responsibilities is adolescence.
Hypothesis	A specific statement about behavior or mental processes that is testable through research is a hypothesis.
Stages	Stages represent relatively discrete periods of time in which functioning is qualitatively different from functioning at other periods.
Acquisition	Acquisition is the process of adapting to the environment, learning or becoming conditioned. In classical conditoning terms, it is the initial learning of the stimulus response link, which involves a neutral stimulus being associated with a unconditioned stimulus and becoming a conditioned stimulus.
Variability	Statistically, variability refers to how much the scores in a distribution spread out, away from the mean.
Variable	A variable refers to a measurable factor, characteristic, or attribute of an individual or a system.
Task analysis	The procedure of identifying the component elements of a behavior chain is called task analysis.
Physical therapy	Physical therapy is a health profession concerned with the assessment, diagnosis, and treatment of disease and disability through physical means. It is based upon principles of medical science, and is generally held to be within the sphere of conventional medicine.
Authentic assessment	Authentic assessment means evaluating a student 's knowledge or skill in a context that approximates the real world or real life as closely as possible .

Learning	Learning is a relatively permanent change in behavior that results from experience. Thus, to attribute a behavioral change to learning, the change must be relatively permanent and must result from experience.
Scheme	According to Piaget, a hypothetical mental structure that permits the classification and organization of new information is called a scheme.
Developmental level	An individual's current state of physical, emotional, and intellectual development is called the developmental level.
Critical thinking	Critical thinking is a mental process of analyzing or evaluating information, particularly statements or propositions that are offered as true.
Acquisition	Acquisition is the process of adapting to the environment, learning or becoming conditioned. In classical conditoning terms, it is the initial learning of the stimulus response link, which involves a neutral stimulus being associated with a unconditioned stimulus and becoming a conditioned stimulus.
Cognitive development	The process by which a child's understanding of the world changes as a function of age and experience is called cognitive development.
Affective	Affective is the way people react emotionally, their ability to feel another living thing's pain or joy.
Accommodation	Piaget's developmental process of accommodation is the modification of currently held schemes or new schemes so that new information inconsistent with the existing schemes can be integrated and understood.
Stages	Stages represent relatively discrete periods of time in which functioning is qualitatively different from functioning at other periods.
Goal-directed behavior	Goal-directed behavior is means-end problem solving behavior. In the infant, such behavior is first observed in the latter part of the first year.
Distinctive features	The characteristics of an object that differentiate it from other objects are distinctive features.
Elaboration	The extensiveness of processing at any given level of memory is called elaboration. The use of elaboration changes developmentally. Adolescents are more likely to use elaboration spontaneously than children.
Population	Population refers to all members of a well-defined group of organisms, events, or things.

Printed in the United Kingdom
by Lightning Source UK Ltd.
117981UK00001B/21